THE 1613 PRINT
of
JUAN ESQUIVEL BARAHONA
Robert J. Snow

Anno M. DC. XIII.

DETROIT MONOGRAPHS IN MUSICOLOGY ❧ NUMBER SEVEN

Information Coordinators, Inc. ❧ 1978 ❧ Detroit

Copyright ©1978 by Robert J. Snow

Printed and bound in the United States of America

Library of Congress Catalog Card Number 78-70021

International Standard Book Number 0-911772-92-8

Published by

Information Coordinators, Inc.

1435-37 Randolph Street, Detroit, Michigan 48226

Book design by Vincent Kibildis

music

CONTENTS

THE 1613 PRINT OF JUAN ESQUIVEL BARAHONA

BECAUSE OF THE RELATIVELY LATE INTRODUCTION of music printing into the Iberian Peninsula and because of the limited number of music printers active there, even as late as the beginning of the seventeenth century, only a small portion of the music composed in Renaissance Spain appeared in print.[1] And because much of the liturgical music composed at that time continued to be used well into the nineteenth century and in some churches even into the twentieth, most of the printed books containing any of this repertory eventually wore out and were replaced by manuscript copies written more often than not on parchment, a much more durable material than the paper of the prints. Consequently, only a small number of copies of most Spanish prints of Spanish Renaissance liturgical music are still in existence. Therefore, the recent discovery of a copy of a print of this period, no copies of which were thought to be preserved, is a matter of some importance for the history of Spanish music.

The print in question is the volume of psalms, hymns, Magnificat settings, Marian antiphons, masses and miscellaneous items by Juan Esquivel Barahona that was published at Salamanca in 1613 by Francisco de Cea Tesa. It is one of the largest collections of Renaissance polyphony ever printed but our knowledge of it has until now been limited solely to the description given of it at the end of the last century by Felipe Pedrell in the entry on Esquivel in his *Diccionario biográfico y bibliográfico de músicos españoles.*[2] Pedrell himself, however, never saw an exemplar of the work. Rather, he knew it only through a copy of the title page, approbation, printing license, dedication and table of contents sent to him by a friend who, he said, also sent him a copy of various pieces in the book. Presumably these were the *Missa pro defunctis* and related items with which the publication concludes since a copy of these, written in a hand other than that of Pedrell, is preserved among the manuscripts constituting the *Legado Pedrell* in the Biblioteca Central in Barcelona.[3]

---

[1] For a useful but somewhat incomplete and by no means error-free list of the music published in Spain in the fifteenth, sixteenth and seventeenth centuries, see Higino Anglès, "Der Musiknotendruck des 15.-17. Jahrhunderts in Spanien," *Musik und Verlag. Karl Vötterle zum 65. Geburtstag,* ed. Richard Baum and Wolfgang Rehm (Kassel: Barenreiter, 1968), pp. 143-49.

[2] Barcelona: Imprenta de Victor Berdos y Feliu, 1894-1897. Unfortunately only the first volume, A-F, and the first fascicule, G-Gaz, of the second volume were published.

[3] See Higino Anglès, *Cataleg dels manuscrits musicals de la col·lecció Pedrell* (Barcelona: Institut d'Estudis Catalans, 1921), pp. 25-26.

Pedrell published all of the textual material he received from his friend in the entry on Esquivel in his *Diccionario.* He chose, however, to give not only Esquivel's dedicatory letter but also the title page, both of which originally were in Latin, in a Spanish translation and thus made it impossible for the reader to ascertain exactly what the original title was. He or his friend also made an error in copying the index and this, plus the failure to include the page numbers of the index in the *Diccionario,* has led certain later scholars to make some erroneous assumptions about the contents of the print, as will be seen below.

Unfortunately, Pedrell did not reveal the name of his friend nor did he disclose the location of the print; perhaps he feared another would study it before he had an opportunity to do so. Whatever his reason, the secret of the name of the friend and of the location of the book died with him. Because no copy of the publication was found by Higino Anglès, who, according to his article on Esquivel in *Die Musik in Geschichte und Gegenwart,* made a year-long search throughout Spain for manuscript copies of Esquivel's music, it generally has been assumed that not only the exemplar indirectly known to Pedrell but any others that might have survived into the present century were all destroyed during the Spanish Civil War or the period of unrest immediately preceding it, when many churches were looted and their contents burned.

Nevertheless, in the summer of 1973 a copy was discovered by the present writer during the course of a visit to Ronda, an ancient city situated some sixty miles west of Malaga. It is preserved there in the sacristy of the church of Santa María de la Encarnación, sometimes referred to as Santa María la Mayor but more often spoken of by the inhabitants of Ronda as "la catedral" because at the time of its construction immediately after the capture of the city from the Moors in 1485 it was destined to be the seat of a bishop. When, however, the person who was to have been the first incumbent of the see died before he had taken possession of his diocese, the area which was to have formed the diocese of Ronda, previously a titular bishopric, was incorporated into neighboring dioceses and Santa María de la Encarnación became a collegiate church rather than a cathedral.[4] In the nineteenth century it was reduced to parochial status and today it is staffed by but a single priest. Its early Baroque organ was destroyed during the time of troubles in the 1930s and only the volume of music by Esquivel remains of what once must have been a rather substantial library of polyphonic works. This volume, along with some dozen or so Renaissance chant books also housed in the sacristy of the church, escaped destruction at that time only because the present sacristan, then an altar boy, succeeded in hiding them before the church was looted.[5]

BIOGRAPHICAL DATA

Even a cursory glance at the music of Esquivel reveals that he was one of the best of the Spanish composers of the late Renaissance, but the musicological literature dealing with him and his music[6] tells us nothing certain concerning his life other than what can be gleaned from his three known publications. The earliest

---

[4] See Carlos Ramón Fort, *Los obispos españoles titulares de iglesias in partibus infidelium.* España Sagrada, 51 (Madrid: Imprenta de José Rodriguez, 1879), 244-45. For general information concerning Ronda, see *Diccionario enciclopédico Hispano-Americano de literatura, ciencias y artes,* 1887-1898, s.v. "Ronda".

[5] This information was communicated *viva voce* by the sacristan.

[6] Only three writers since Pedrell have dealt with Esquivel and his music other than in the most cursory manner: Albert Geiger, "Juan Esquivel. Ein unbekannter spanischer Meister des 16. Jahrhunderts," *Festschrift zum 50. Geburtstag Adolf Sandberger* (Munich: Ferdinand Zierfuss, 1918), pp. 138-69; Higino Anglès, *Die Musik in Geschichte und Gegenwart,* s.v. "Esquivel (Barahona), Juan"; Robert M. Stevenson, *Spanish Cathedral Music in the Golden Age* (Berkeley: University of California Press, 1961), pp. 288-97.

of these was a collection of masses published in 1608, the second a volume of motets dating from the same year and the third the volume under consideration here.[7] The title page of the 1613 print, reproduced on page 11, states that he was a native of Ciudad Rodrigo—"Civitatensis" is the adjectival form of the Latin name for Ciudad Rodrigo—and that he was a prebendary of the cathedral there at the time the license to print was issued. The approbation and license to print add that he also was chapelmaster. From the title page of the 1608 volume of masses, known only from the article by Albert Geiger cited in footnote 6, we learn that he already held his prebend and the chapelmastership early in 1608. The dedicatory letter of the 1613 print reveals that one of his patrons was a former bishop of Ciudad Rodrigo, Pedro Ponce de León.

Three different forms of his name appear in sources contemporary with him and two others are to be found in current musicological literature. The form which he favored seems to have been Juan Esquivel since in the titles of all three of his known publications he is called simply Joannes Esquivel and this is the form by which he refers to himself in the dedicatory letter in the 1613 print. In the approbation and the printing license of this volume, however, he is referred to respectively as Juan and Joan de Esquivel Barahona and, according to Pedrell's article on Vicente Espinel in his *Diccionario,* the form Juan Gil de Esquivel Barahona was used by Juan Pérez de Guzmán, the biographer of Espinel. The two forms to be found in current musicological literature are Juan Barahona de Esquivel, used by Rafael Mitjana in his study on Spanish music in the *Encyclopédie de la musique et dictionnaire du Conservatoire,*[8] and Juan Esquivel de Barahona, which is used for the unsigned entry for this composer in the *Diccionario de la música Labor*[9] and in the *Répertoire international des sources musicales (RISM),* Series A/I. In all probability the correct full form of his name was Juan Esquivel Barahona, with Esquivel being the family name of his father and Barahona that of his mother. The use of "de" in the approbation and the license to print must have been nothing more than a mark of courtesy. It is not known on what basis Espinel's biographer added "Gil" and the forms used by Mitjana and in the *Diccionario de la música Labor* and *RISM* seem to have no basis in fact and probably resulted from carelessness on the part of the various writers.

Unfortunately, the capitular acts of the cathedral of Ciudad Rodrigo have been destroyed for the years 1569 through 1642; only a few loose pages dealing with isolated acts from 1598, 1599 and 1600 have been preserved and none of these deals with musical matters. Important information concerning Esquivel as well as several of his predecessors at Ciudad Rodrigo has, however, been preserved in a history of the cathedral which was written early in the seventeenth century by one Antonio Sánchez Cabañas, a choir chaplain at the cathedral of Ciudad Rodrigo during Esquivel's tenure of office. A summary of this information plus information extracted from capitular acts prior to 1569, is presented on pages 289-94 of the first of the two volumes constituting the history of the cathedral and the city of Ciudad Rodrigo by Mateo Hernández Vegas, *Ciudad Rodrigo. La catedral y la ciudad.*[10] According to Hernández Vegas, Sánchez Cabañas states that Esquivel was a native of Ciudad Rodrigo, served as a choirboy at the cathedral there and was a student of Juan Navarro when this composer served as the cathedral's chapelmaster.[11] He further states that Esquivel

---

[7]For information concerning the two prints of 1608, see Appendix II, pp. 93-95.

[8]Albert Lavignac and Lionel de la Laurencie, ed. (Paris: Librairie Delagrave, 1913-1931), I/4: 2042.

[9]Joaquin Pena, Higino Anglès et al. (Barcelona: Editorial Labor, 1954). It should be noted that this entry contains several errors, including the statement that Esquivel was chapelmaster at the cathedral in Salamanca in 1608, an error which is repeated in Anglès's entry in *Die Musik in Geschichte und Gegenwart.*

[10]Salamanca: Imprenta Comercial Salmantina, 1935.

[11]Concerning Juan Navarro, see Robert M. Stevenson, *Die Musik in Geschichte und Gegenwart,* s.v. "Navarro, Juan." In his *Spanish Cathedral Music,* p. 288, Stevenson states that Esquivel studied with this composer but gives no evidence to support his assertion.

gained each post for which he competed, the first of these having been that of chapelmaster at Oviedo. From Oviedo he is said to have moved to Calahorra and then to Avila before returning home to assume the directorship at Ciudad Rodrigo, where he remained until his death.

Hernández Vegas gives no dates for Esquivel's term of office at Ciudad Rodrigo; perhaps Sánchez Cabañas himself gave none. In any case, it is clear from remarks of Hernández Vegas that the history by Sánchez Cabañas and the capitular acts prior to 1569 contain more information about musical activities at Ciudad Rodrigo than he presented in his summary. Consequently these sources need to be examined not only for additional information about Esquivel and his music but also for any light they may shed on important earlier figures such as Giraldin Bucher and his son, Diego Bucher (who also were known as Buxer, Buxel and Bujel), Juan Cepa, Zuñeda, Juan Navarro, Alonso de Velasco and Alonso de Tejeda, all of whom are mentioned by Hernández Vegas as having been among the predecessors of Esquivel at Ciudad Rodrigo.[12] Also, an examination of the municipal archives, much richer and better preserved than those of the cathedral, and those of the episcopal palace and various parochial and collegiate churches and religious houses of Ciudad Rodrigo, as well as those of the other cities where Esquivel worked, might yield still more information about this little-known but unquestionably important Spanish composer of the late Renaissance.

DESCRIPTION OF THE PRINT

Esquivel's publication of 1613 consists of 593 numbered pages plus four unnumbered ones at the beginning and a single unnumbered one at the end. The first of the four pages without number at the beginning of the book is the title page, the second is blank, the third contains the approbation and the printing license, and the fourth the dedication. The unnumbered page at the end of the book, the verso of page 593, contains the colophon. The index occurs on page 1, and pages 2 through 593 all have music.

The copy preserved in Ronda is bound between the usual leather-covered boards and is in an excellent state of preservation. Although the pages were trimmed at least once when the book was bound or rebound and now measure only 52 cm in height by 37 cm in width, no music has been cut off and the repairs made to pages 2 through 14 and to a few others scattered throughout the volume were done with such care that only a half-dozen or so notes have been obscured. The loss, however, of the lower outer corner of the second leaf of the book (shown on page 13), which contains the third and the fourth of the unnumbered pages, has resulted in the disappearance of part of the family name of the official by whose order the license was issued. The complete name of this person is preserved, however, in the copy of the license given by Pedrell.

The title of the print, as can be seen on page 11, is: *Ioannis Esquivel, Civitatensis et eiusdem sanctae ecclesiae portionarii, psalmorum, hymnorum, Magnificarum et b. Mariae quatuor antiphonarum de*

---

[12] Because of the importance of the information which Hernández Vegas gives and because copies of his history apparently are to be found in only two libraries in the United States, neither of which permits the work to circulate on interlibrary loan, the entire passage is reproduced in Appendix III, pp. 97-98. If Alonso de Tejeda was Esquivel's immediate predecessor, as Hernández Vegas seems to suggest, Esquivel probably began his service at Ciudad Rodrigo in the summer or fall of 1591 since Tejeda was elected chapelmaster of the cathedral of León in February of that year and left Ciudad Rodrigo shortly thereafter; see Dionisio Preciado, *Alonso de Tejeda* (Madrid: Editorial Alpuerto, 1974), p. 22.

IOANNIS, ESQVIVEL, CIVITATENSIS,

ET EIVSDEM SANCTAE ECCLESIAE PORTIONARII,

PSALMORVM, HYMNORVM, MAGNIFICARVM, ET ?.
MARIÆ QVATVOR ANTIPHONARVM DE
TEMPORE, NECNON ET MISSARVM

TOMVS SECVNDVS.

Omnia ad vſum Breuiarij Romani per Clementem Pontificem
Maximum reformati.

AD PRÆSTANTISSIMVM, ET REVERENDISSIMVM
DOMINVM FRATREM D. PETRVM PONTIVM DE LEON
ÇAMORENSEM EPISCOPVM, REGIVMQVE
CONSILIARIVM.

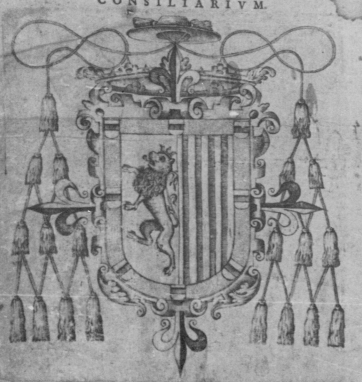

SVPERIORVM PERMISSV.

SALMANTICÆ

Excudebat Franciscvs de Cea Tesa Cordubensis
Anno M. DC. XIII.

Title page of
the 1613 print of
Esquivel.

tempore, necnon et missarum tomus secundus.[13] The inclusion of such a large variety of music for use in the Mass and Office Hours in a single volume, whether a print or a manuscript, is somewhat unusual in Spain and not infrequently even Magnificat settings appear apart from those of psalms and hymns even though all are for the same Office Hour. This suggests that the volume consists of what originally were three separate collections of music and this is confirmed by the approbation, the license and the index. Vicente Espinel, who gave the approbation on December 7, 1611, says "vi tres cuerpos de Musica"[14] and Martín de Córdova, who granted the license, speaks of "tres libros que [Joan de Esquivel Barahona] ha compuesto de musica, uno de Missas, otro de Magnificas, y otro de Hymnos, y Salmos." (See page 13.) The index, in turn, as can be seen on page 15, seems to indicate three separate collections by re-using the word "Index" before listing the Magnificat settings and again before the masses.

The fact that the volume does indeed consist of what originally were three separate and distinct units provides a possible answer to a somewhat puzzling aspect of the title. Literally translated it reads: *The Second Volume of Psalms, Hymns, Magnificat Settings and the Four Seasonal Marian Antiphons, as well as of Masses, by Juan Esquivel, a native of Ciudad Rodrigo and Prebendary of the Cathedral of the same City.* As mentioned above, the only two previous publications known to contain music by Esquivel are a volume of masses and one of motets, but the title of the 1613 print, if taken literally, would indicate that there was not only an earlier collection of masses but also one of psalms, hymns and Magnificat settings. I would suggest that this was not the case and that the adjective "secundus" should be taken to refer only to the collection of masses. Perhaps the ambiguity of the title arose from the need to compress the titles of the three collections into but a single title when it was decided to issue all three in one volume.[15]

The title page states that the contents conform to the Roman breviary as reformed by Pope Clement VIII: *Omnia ad usum Breviarii Romani per Clementem Pontificem Maximum reformati.* The breviary in question is that which was issued by Clement VIII in 1602 and that the contents of Esquivel's collection conform to this edition is affirmed by Espinel in his approbation. That such conformity was required is evident from the license to print, granted by Martín de Córdova, *Comissario General,* who had the responsibility for ascertaining that all liturgical books conformed to "the new manner of praying." The nature of the conformity required is not stated, but obviously the texts in a collection of this kind and their liturgical assignment would have to be in agreement with those of the breviary then in use.

Interestingly, textual conformity with the breviary of Clement VIII was not the only aspect of the collection that was considered before the license was issued. That the quality of the music and its suitability for liturgical use also were taken into account can be seen both from the approbation and from the license to print. In his approbation, Espinel expressed the opinion that the items in the three books

---

[13]The "et" in the title which occurs between the words "necnon" and "missarum" must not have been clearly written by Pedrell's friend since in his article on Esquivel in the *Diccionario* Pedrell gave it as a "T," the significance of which, he confessed, escaped him.

[14]That Vicente Espinel was not only a native of Ronda and for several years one of the beneficed clergy attached to the church of Santa María de la Encarnación but also one of the city's most illustrious sons may well have been responsible at least to some degree for the preservation of the Esquivel print. In any case, it is precisely Espinel's approbation which gives the volume its importance in the eyes of the present-day personnel at Santa María de la Encarnación. It is not impossible that the volume was presented to the church by Espinel.

[15]Pedrell, who knew neither of the prints from 1608, assumed in his *Diccionario* article that the 1613 print was the second of three publications by Esquivel, these being the "tres cuerpos" spoken of by Espinel in his approbation: "De estos *tres cuerpos* solo ha aparecido el segundo . . ."

APROBACION DEL MAESTRO ESPINEL.

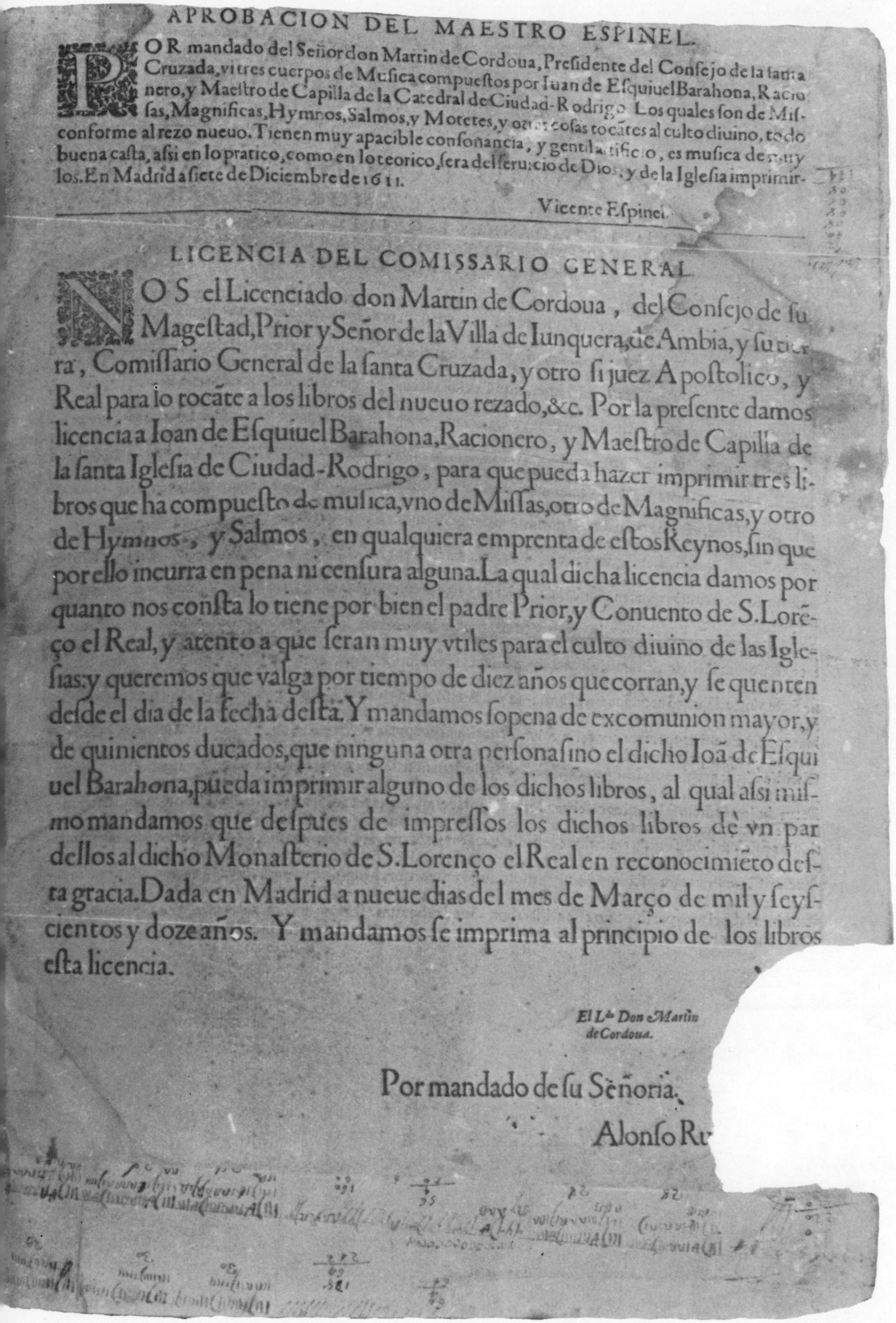

POR mandado del Señor don Martin de Cordoua, Presidente del Consejo de la santa Cruzada, vi tres cuerpos de Musica compuestos por Iuan de Esquiuel Barahona, Racionero, y Maestro de Capilla de la Catedral de Ciudad-Rodrigo. Los quales son de Missas, Magnificas, Hymnos, Salmos, y Motetes, y otras cosas tocãtes al culto diuino, todo conforme al rezo nueuo. Tienen muy apacible consonancia, y gentil artificio, es musica de muy buena casta, assi en lo pratico, como en lo teorico, sera del seruicio de Dios, y de la Iglesia imprimirlos. En Madrid a siete de Diciembre de 1611.

Vicente Espinel.

LICENCIA DEL COMISSARIO GENERAL

NOS el Licenciado don Martin de Cordoua, del Consejo de su Magestad, Prior y Señor de la Villa de Iunquera, de Ambia, y su tierra, Comissario General de la santa Cruzada, y otro si juez Apostolico, y Real para lo tocãte a los libros del nueuo rezado, &c. Por la presente damos licencia a Ioan de Esquiuel Barahona, Racionero, y Maestro de Capilla de la santa Iglesia de Ciudad-Rodrigo, para que pueda hazer imprimir tres libros que ha compuesto de musica, vno de Missas, otro de Magnificas, y otro de Hymnos, y Salmos, en qualquiera emprenta de estos Reynos, sin que por ello incurra en pena ni censura alguna. La qual dicha licencia damos por quanto nos consta lo tiene por bien el padre Prior, y Conuento de S. Lorêço el Real, y atento a que seran muy vtiles para el culto diuino de las Iglesias: y queremos que valga por tiempo de diez años que corran, y se quenten desde el dia de la fecha desta. Y mandamos sopena de excomunion mayor, y de quinientos ducados, que ninguna otra persona sino el dicho Ioã de Esquiuel Barahona, pueda imprimir alguno de los dichos libros, al qual assi mismo mandamos que despues de impressos los dichos libros dè vn par dellos al dicho Monasterio de S. Lorenço el Real en reconocimiẽto desta gracia. Dada en Madrid a nueue dias del mes de Março de mil y seyscientos y doze años. Y mandamos se imprima al principio de los libros esta licencia.

El L.do Don Martin de Cordoua.

Por mandado de su Señoria.

Alonso Ru

Approbation and license of the 1613 print.

PRÆCLARISSIMO DOMINO FRATRI D.

PETRO PONZE DE LEON, CAMORENSI EPISCOPO
DIGNISSIMO, IOANNES ESQVIVEL ALMÆ CIVITA-
TENSIS ECCLESIÆ PORTIONARIVS, MVSI-
CÆQVE PRÆFECTVS S. P. D.

Vperioribus annis cùm ad hanc regédam Ecclesiam, diuina id efficiente gratia, assumptus esses, clarissime Præsul, vniuersùmque populum præcipua quadam amoris significatione tibi concisiasses, me imprimis tua animi mansuetudo, & lenitas sic sibi deuinxit, vt te mihi in omnibus patronum, ac Mecœnatem iam inde elegerim. Cuius obseruantiæ, & gratitudinis specimen aliquod cùm enixè dare optarem, diuturni desiderij finem præsens fecit occasio. Volenti enim mihi volumen quoddam de concentu Ecclesiastico typis mandare, illúdque alicuius Principis præsidio, recepta iam consuetudine, committere, non fuit diutius deliberandum; multæ siquidè se se obtulerunt causæ, quæ me ad patrocinium tuum cæteris anteponendum facilè perpulerunt. Considero namque tuæ familiæ antiquitatem, tuorum progenitorum pro amplificanda Christiana religione à sexcentis annis res benè gestas in mentè reuoco. Quas ex Granatensibus, Africanísq, Mauris victorias feliciter reportauerint historiæ ipsæ haud obscurè manifestant, quibus deniq, prædijs, quibus possessionibus multa Diuorum Templa ditauerint, pia eorum, & religiosa monimenta testatur. Quæ omnia cùm ad veri Dei cultum, suorúmque Regum fidelem operam reuocata esse constet, inde factum est, vt non solùm Archobriga, Zaræ, Martiæ, Gadium, aliorúmque oppidorum dominiú meritò obtinere, verùm etiam Tolosanorum, Narbonensiúmque Comitum insitam nobilitatem felici Legionis, & Aragoniæ Regum affinitate cumulare meruerint. Sed quia hæc in tantis temporum interuallis tam fortè exolera esse possent, mirum est dictu, quanto animi ardore, ac fortitudine his proximis annis excellentissimus Dux Rothericus frater tuus, cæteris totius Bæticæ dynastis timore perterritis, ad pellendos Gadibus perfidos Anglos, Templorum, & sacrarum virginum vlciscendas iniurias fulgerissima suorum subditorum stipatus caterua processerit, ita vt eius accelerationis fama hostes ipsos tantæ virtutis stupore defixos ex pauida, & direpta vrbe potuerit exturbare. Ne autem quis te illis aliqua ex parte inferiorem ignoráter iudicet, diuini numinis instinctu effectum fuisse credo, vt molli, & delicata tunica cilicio, renitente purpura rudi, & aspero Dominicanæ familiæ vestitu commutata, arctiorem Religionis vitam elegeris: ná si illi inter tubarum clangorem, inter armorum strepitum, bombardæque reboatum humanam, atque ideò fluxam, & perituram gloriam, magna Hispanorum Regum Imperio accessione facta, sunt adepti, tu nequaquam his minora præstitisti: cùm enim Regnum Cœlorum vim pati ex assidua sacrarum Literarú lectione didiceris, illud expugnandum ratus, omni virtutum armatura munitus, operi te accinxisti: voluntaria siquidem paupertate contentus, inter continuas corporis verberationes, ciborum abstinentias, indefessas vigilias, propria priuatus voluntate, publicis ad populum concionibus, priuatis confessionum colloquijs, sic tibi, Christianóque gregi consuluisti, vt tuis laboribus gloriam non deficientem in cœlis, & Regi Regum Christo innumeros filios te peperisse nemo dubitet. Cui igitur, cùm hæc vera sint, aptius, consultiúsque mearum lucubrationum fœtus diuino Officio solemnius celebrando multo maiore, quàm antea studio, & diligentia elaboratos, quàm tibi destinare debui, cuius maioribus cultu, & obseruantia Deo omnium largitori debita nihil vnquam aut charius, aut antiquius fuisse minimè dubia traditione accepimus, & qui totam vitæ seriem, cunctásque actiones sic semper instituisti, vt Orthodoxæ fidei augmento, & propagationi, de tuæ Religionis more, indefesse inseruieris. Suscipe igitur, præclarissime Præsul, opusculum hoc Psalmorum, Hymnorum, Magnificarum, & Missarum modulos pro sui authoris tenuitate complectens, quod si sub amplissimi tui nominis protectione prodire patieris, satis cumulatum præmium labori meo persolutum esse arbitror. Quod reliquum est Dominationem tuam Deus Optimus Maximus ad sui nominis gloriam, Ecclesiǽque ornamentum quam diutissimè tueatur incolumen.

Dedicatory letter
of the 1613 print.
See page ninety-one.

14

INDEX OMNIVM, QVÆ IN HOC
VOLVMINE CONTINENTVR.

Index.

"tienen muy apacible consonancia, y gentil artificio, es musica de muy buena casta, assi en lo practico, como en lo teorico, sera del servicio de Dios y de la Iglesia imprimirlos." And from the license it can be seen that a further opinion was secured from the prior and members of the royal monastery at El Escorial: "La qual dicha licencia damos por quanto nos consta lo tiene por bien el padre Prior, y Convento de S. Lorenzo el Real, y atento a que seran muy utiles para el culto divino de las Iglesias."

The license was issued at Madrid on March 9, 1612, and permitted Esquivel to have his "tres libros" printed by any printer in the kingdom. It also protected his rights to the music for a period of ten years and imposed not only the severe penalty of excommunication but also a fine of 500 ducats, no small sum, on anyone else who dared to print any of it within that period of time. The license appears, of course, above the name of Martín de Córdova, but in reality it was issued by the order of one Alonso Ruyz, a lesser official, part of whose family name was on that portion of the page now torn away in the Ronda copy, as can be seen on page 13. As mentioned above, the full name has been preserved only in the copy of the license as printed by Pedrell in his *Diccionario*.

The printer whom Esquivel chose was Francisco de Cea Tesa, a native of Cordoba who probably had established his business in Salamanca because of the presence of a university there. According to the colophon, the book was completed on February 25, 1613, a few days less than a year after the issuance of the license to print: *Salmanticae excudebat Franciscus de Cea Tesa Cordubensis, quinto kalendas Martias anni M. DC. XIII.*

The license to print is followed by the dedicatory letter to Pedro Ponce de León, whose coat of arms appears on the title page immediately below the lines of dedication there. See page 14.[16] At the time Esquivel completed work on his 1613 collection this prelate, a Dominican, was bishop of Zamora, but his first episcopal appointment had been at Ciudad Rodrigo, where he served from 1605 to 1610. Rector of the University of Salamanca prior to his episcopal consecration, he came from one of the most illustrious of the great Andalusian families. His father was Luis Cristóbal Ponce de León, Duke of Arcos, who had played the role of Maecenas to musicians by his liberality to Morales, whom he employed as his chapelmaster at Marchena from 1548 to 1551, and, after Morales's death, to Guerrero, who dedicated to him his *Sacrae cantiones* of 1555. From Esquivel's Latin dedicatory epistle to Don Pedro it seems that this prelate had befriended the composer while he was bishop of Ciudad Rodrigo and Esquivel was his chapelmaster, and that by his patronage he perhaps had made possible the publication of Esquivel's two prints of 1608. It is impossible to say, however, whether or not either of these two earlier books was dedicated to the bishop because all preserved copies of them have lost those pages which would have contained dedicatory material.[17]

The index of the 1613 print, reproduced on page 15, occurs on the first of the series of numbered pages. It is headed with the superscription *Index omnium quae in hoc volumine continentur* and contains

---

[16]Because of the smallness of the print in the illustration on page 14, the text of the dedicatory letter is given in Appendix I, pp. 91-92.

[17]The various Spanish reference works dealing with this prelate and the bishopric of Ciudad Rodrigo give conflicting dates for his occupancy of the see. The most recent of these, *Diccionario de historia eclesiastica de España* (Madrid: Instituto Enrique Flórez, 1972-   ), s.v. "Ciudad Rodrigo," gives the dates of his incumbency as August 13, 1605-February 4, 1610, but earlier works state that he was translated to the see of Zamora in 1609. In either case, he had been bishop of Ciudad Rodrigo for almost three years when Esquivel's two collections of 1608 were published.

eighty entries arranged in two columns. The contents are divided into seven groups, each of which, except for the fifth, has its own subheading. Groups 1 and 2 contain psalms and hymns respectively and undoubtedly constitute one of the "tres cuerpos" or "tres libros" spoken of in the approbation and license. Group 3, the subheading of which contains the word "Index," consists of Magnificat settings and along with group 4 it must have formed another of the original three books. The third book surely consisted of groups 6 and 7 and again the heading of the sixth group contains the word "Index." These two groups contain, respectively, mass ordinaries and a *Missa pro defunctis* and related material, just as did the 1608 volume of masses. Of the miscellaneous items in group 5, one is for use in Matins and another in Lauds whereas the other three are for use in connection with the Mass liturgy. In Esquivel's original arrangement some of these probably were attached to the second of the three books and some to the third.

CONTENTS OF THE PRINT

Psalms. The group of nine items with which the volume begins is entitled *Psalmi omnes quatuor vocum* in the index but this heading is not completely correct because the last of the items is not a psalm. Rather, it is the canticle sung at Compline, *Nunc dimittis,* and is one of the two items which Esquivel provided for this evening Office Hour, the other being the hymn *Te lucis ante terminum,* with which the cycle of hymns concludes. Verses 2 and 4 of this canticle are composed for the customary SATB combination of voices but verse 6, "Sicut erat," is set for six voices. The musical treatment accorded this canticle is similar in all respects to that which usually is applied to Office psalms rather than to canticles. It is written in tone 8, as is customary in the Spanish tradition, and the psalm-tone formula is present in one or another voice in each of the verses. In verse 2 it appears in the tenor, in verse 4 it is in the superius and in verse 6 it is assigned to the superius primus.

The other eight items are psalms for Vespers. Only seven different texts are set, however, since one, *Dixit Dominus,* appears twice, once in tone 1 and once in tone 6, as can be seen in Table I, *below,* which lists the psalms and indicates the tone of each as well as which verses are set for any combination of voices other than the customary one of SATB.

TABLE I

PSALM SETTINGS

PSALM	TONE	VERSES OTHER THAN SATB
1. Dixit Dominus (109)	1	8. De torrente; SSTB
2. Beatus vir (111)	4	
3. Laudate Dominum (116)	8	
4. Dixit Dominus (109)	6	8. De torrente; SAT 10. Sicut erat; SSATB
5. Laetatus sum (121)	3	10. Gloria Patri; SSATB
6. Lauda Jerusalem (147)	7	10. Gloria Patri; SSATB
7. Credidi (115)	5	
8. In exitu Israel (113)	Peregrinus	29. Sicut erat; SSAB

The musical treatment of these psalms conforms to the traditions of the time. Each of the even-numbered verses of the first seven of them receives an individualized setting which is shaped by the prosody of the text. In each of these the psalm-tone formula appears in one or another voice-part in a more or less recognizable form and as a rule it is treated more freely in the later verses of a psalm than in the earlier ones. As is evident from Table I, page 17, almost all verses are for the usual SATB combination of voices. Only in the doxological verse of three of the settings is the number of voices increased to five; perhaps it is significant that all three of these psalms are sung at Marian Vespers. For an illustration of these various aspects, see Example 1, which consists of the setting of *Dixit Dominus* in tone 6, pages 39-42.

The treatment of the eighth psalm, *In exitu Israel*, differs from that accorded the first seven but it also falls within the tradition of the time. Here all of the verses except the last are sung to a single falsobordone formula; thus, only the doxological verse receives an individualized setting. Also, in this psalm the odd-numbered rather than the even-numbered verses must have been sung polyphonically since verse 1 rather than verse 2 is underlaid to the formula and it is "Sicut erat," verse 29, rather than "Gloria Patri," verse 28, which receives individualized polyphonic treatment.

At first glance Esquivel's collection of psalms seems to be very incomplete since it includes settings of only seven of the sixteen used in First and Second Vespers on feasts of duplex rank in the temporal and sanctoral cycles and in Sunday Vespers. Moreover, except for *Dixit Dominus,* it provides a setting in only one tone for each of these. A careful consideration of the psalms constituting the cycle reveals, however, that at least from the textual standpoint the collection is indeed a complete one because it is evident from the psalms which the composer included that his intention was to provide polyphony only for the first, the third and the fifth of those used in First Vespers on feasts of duplex rank and at Sunday Vespers. Thus, his first three psalms, *Dixit Dominus, Beatus vir* and *Laudate Dominum,* are the first, third and fifth of those sung in First Vespers on all of the greater feasts of the temporal cycle, except those of the Circumcision and Corpus Christi, and on all feasts of male saints and of angels. The next three, *Dixit Dominus, Laetatus sum* and *Lauda Jerusalem,* are the first, third and fifth of those sung in First Vespers on all Marian feasts and on the feasts of all other female saints, as well as on the feast of the Circumcision and the Purification. Furthermore, *Dixit Dominus, Beatus vir* and *Lauda Jerusalem* are the first, third and fifth of those sung in First Vespers on feasts celebrating the dedication of a church whereas *Dixit Dominus, Credidi* and *Lauda Jerusalem* are the first, third and fifth used in First Vespers of Corpus Christi and *Dixit Dominus, Beatus vir* and *In exitu Israel* are the first, third and fifth of those always sung at Vespers on Sunday.

All of these psalms except *In exitu Israel,* are, of course, also used as the first, third or fifth of the psalms sung in Second Vespers on several of the same feasts, but since Esquivel did not include in his cycle any of the three additional ones which sometimes appear as the fifth of those sung in Second Vespers on certain feasts in both the temporal and sanctoral cycles but never in First Vespers—*Memento Domine* (131), *Confitebor tibi* (137) and *Domine probasti me* (138)—it is probable that he intended his collection for use only in First Vespers. Perhaps in Second Vespers at Ciudad Rodrigo all five psalms were sung monophonically or the first, third and fifth were sung to simple falsobordone formulas. The second and fourth psalms probably were always sung monophonically at both Vespers in order not to prolong the service unduly.

Without access to the manuscript chant books in use at Ciudad Rodrigo in the early seventeenth century it is impossible to ascertain for which specific feasts, if any, Esquivel composed the psalms which he included in his print of 1613. By about 1575 almost all Spanish dioceses had accepted the liturgical reforms embodied in the missal and breviary of Pius V and from that time on Spanish churches essentially conformed to Roman usage in such basic things as textual assignment, rubrics, calendar and so forth. In musical matters, however, dioceses and religious houses throughout Spain adhered to their traditional practices whenever this was possible. Consequently, Spanish graduals and, particularly, antiphonaries often differed considerably from their Roman counterparts in their choice of melodies for use with antiphon and hymn texts as well as for the tones used by the celebrant of the Mass and for the singing of the Passion, the Lamentations of Jeremiah and the *Exsultet,* for example. Only in the nineteenth century did Spanish musical practices gradually begin to come into conformity with those of Rome. This was one of the results of the increasing influence of the Order of St. Francis, the liturgical books of which were based primarily on Roman musical as well as liturgical customs.

Hymns. A cycle of thirty hymns for Vespers, to which is appended the Compline hymn, *Te lucis ante terminum,* follows the psalms.[18] The hymns for the temporal cycle and those proper to individual saints are intermixed and presented in an order which conforms, for the most part, to that of the liturgical year and are followed by the hymns common to many saints. The exact order in which they occur can be seen in Table II, page 20, which lists the liturgical occasions for which hymns are given and the title of the hymn provided for each of these. The strophes which receive polyphonic treatment and the voices used, as well as the total number of strophes comprising each hymn, also are indicated.

The hymns constituting the cycle are precisely those which are sung at Vespers on feasts which in the breviary of Clement VIII had duplex rank. The texts of two of the hymns, however, are not to be found in the main body of this breviary; rather, they occur in a supplement containing propers for feasts peculiar to Spanish usage. One of these is the hymn for the feast of St. James, the patron saint of Spain, and the other is the hymn for the feast of Guardian Angels, which long had been celebrated throughout Spain but did not yet enjoy Roman usage at the time the breviary of Clement VIII was printed.

Esquivel normally set either one or two of the even-numbered strophes of each hymn. Never did he provide settings for more than two even when the total number of these exceeded five. Consequently, if all of the even-numbered strophes of many of the hymns were ever sung polyphonically from Esquivel's collection, two strophes would have had to be sung to the same music. There is, however, no indication in the print that this was to be done. In this matter Esquivel's hymn cycle stands midway between the practice of the greater part of the sixteenth century, when each alternate strophe was provided with its own setting, and that which prevailed from about the middle of the seventeenth century on, when sources usually give polyphony for but a single strophe. In only two instances did Esquivel set odd-numbered strophes and in both cases, strophe 1 of the setting of *Vexilla Regis* for Passion Sunday and Palm Sunday, and strophe 5 of *Pange lingua,* for Corpus Christi, he was only following Spanish custom, which traditionally emphasized these strophes by setting them polyphonically.

As also can be seen in Table II, in only three instances is a strophe set for a combination of voices other than the usual one of SATB and no canonic device is ever employed. Each setting, however, incorporates in one way or another the traditional chant melody to which each hymn was sung. Usually this melody appears in its entirety in a slightly modified form in one voice or another or is divided between different voices and may or may not be treated imitatively, as can be seen in Example 2, *Veni Creator Spiritus,* pages 43-45.

---

[18] Only twenty-nine of the thirty liturgical occasions for which Vespers hymns are provided appear in Pedrell's presentation of the index in his *Diccionario.* Either he or his friend made an error in copying it and combined the twenty-sixth and twenty-seventh occasions, *Plurimorum martyrum* and *Confessorum pontificum,* into but a single one reading *Plurimorum pontificum.*

TABLE II
HYMN SETTINGS

FEAST	TITLE	STROPHES SET	TOTAL NO. OF STROPHES
1. In Adventu Domini	Conditor alme siderum	2, 4	6
2. In Nativitate Domini	Christe Redemptor omnium, Ex Patre	2, 4 (SAT)	7
3. Sanctorum Innocentium	Salvete flores Martyrum	2	3
4. In Epiphania Domini	Hostis Herodes impie	2, 4	5
5. Angeli Custodis	Custodes hominum	2, 4	4
6. Dominicae in Passione	Vexilla Regis prodeunt	1, 6	7
7. Dominicae in Albis	Ad coenam Agni providi	2, 8	8
8. In festis S. Crucis	Vexilla Regis prodeunt	2, 6	7
9. S. Michaelis	Tibi Christe splendor Patris	2	4
10. In Ascensione Domini	Jesu nostra redemptio	2, 4	6
11. In festo Pentecostes	Veni Creator Spiritus	2, 4 (SST)	7
12. In festo sanctissimae Trinitatis	O lux beata Trinitas	2	3
13. In festo Corporis Christi	Pange lingua gloriosi	2, 5 (SSAT)	7
14. In Nativitate S. Joannis Baptistae	Ut quaeant laxis	2, 4	5
15. In festo Apostolorum Petri et Pauli	Aurea luce	2	4
16. S. Mariae Magdalenae	Pater superni luminis	2, 4	5
17. S. Jacobi Apostoli	Defensor alme Hispaniae	2, 4	7
18. Petri ad Vincula	Petrus beatus	2	2
19. Transfigurationis Domini	Quicumque Christum quaeritis	2, 4	5
20. In festis Virginis Mariae	Ave maris stella	2, 4	7
21. Omnium Sanctorum	Christe Redemptor omnium, Conserva	2, 4	7
22. Conversionis S. Pauli	Doctor egregie Paule	2	2
23. Commune Apostolorum	Exsultet caelum laudibus	2	6
24. Commune Apostolorum tempore Paschali	Tristes erant Apostoli	2, 6	6
25. Unius Martyris	Deus tuorum militum	2	5
26. Plurimorum Martyrum	Sanctorum meritis	2	6
27. Confessorum Pontificum	Iste confessor	2	5
28. Virginum	Jesu corona virginum	2	5
29. Pro nec Virgine nec Martyre	Fortem virili pectore	2, 4	5
30. Dedicationis Ecclesiae	Urbs beata Jerusalem	2, 4	5
31. Ad Completorum	Te lucis ante terminum	2	3

In his choice of pre-existent material Esquivel followed, of course, the Spanish tradition, which for a number of hymns used melodies other than those customary in other areas of Europe. Among these melodies are several which were in a strict triple meter in their monophonic form and it is interesting to note that Esquivel, as did most Spanish composers, preserved this feature of these chants in his polyphonic settings of them by casting the music in a definitely triple meter and notating it under the mensural sign O3. One such hymn is *Pater supernis luminis,* for the feast of St. Mary Magdalen, which is given as Example 3, pages 46-48. Here the original chant melody is slightly modified and presented in the superius of strophe 2 whereas in strophe 4 it is modified a bit more, transposed to the lower fourth and assigned to the altus.

Magnificat Settings. The sixteen Magnificat settings which constitute the third section of the print are grouped into two cycles, each of which contains eight settings of this canticle, one in each of the eight tones. The first cycle consists of settings of the odd-numbered verses and the second of the even-numbered ones. Both in the index and in the body of the book, the settings that contain odd-numbered verses are designated for use at First Vespers and those that contain even-numbered verses are assigned to Second Vespers. This is welcome information since it is one of the rare instances of direct evidence concerning the specific liturgical assignment of Magnificat settings of odd- and even-numbered verses. It should not, however, be assumed that the assignment specified here was necessarily the general practice of the entire Renaissance; there is too much indirect evidence suggesting that the practice in this matter varied from time to time and place to place.

The general musical characteristics of the Magnificat settings are typical of their time. It should be noted, however, that although many verses utilize the corresponding canticle tone either as a kind of cantus firmus or as a source for motival material, not all of them do so, and when the canticle tone is absent it is from one or another of the later verses of a setting rather than from an earlier one. Also, the two cycles differ considerably from each other in regard to the degree of musical elaborateness accorded their settings and, as one would expect, it was on the settings of odd-numbered verses—destined for use at First Vespers, a liturgical service of slightly higher rank than Second Vespers—that Esquivel lavished his compositional skills. In so doing, he undoubtedly was seeking to emulate Sebastián de Vivanco who, in his *Liber Magnificarum* of 1607, also published in Salamanca, had created a veritable compendium of the contrapuntal devices of the time.

As can be seen in Table III, page 23, which gives the number of voices indicated in the index for each setting of the odd-numbered verses as well as the voices actually used in each verse of these and the canons by which voices are to be derived, over forty percent of the verses are for more than four voices and from one to four parts are derived canonically not only in all except one of the doxological verses but also in two of the internal verses. In the settings of even-numbered verses, however, for use at Second Vespers, only four verses—the "Sicut erat" of tones 2, 5, 6 and 7—are set for more than four voices and in only one, the "Sicut erat" of tone 5, is a part canonically derived. There the tenor secundus is derived from the altus according to the canon *Quod ascendit descendit, in diapente.* Interestingly, none of the canonically derived parts is notated; Esquivel always left it to the singers to derive them at the moment of performance. Contrapuntal devices other than those used in creating canonically derived parts are, of course, employed at various places in the settings and a madrigalesque kind of word-painting is to be found occasionally, as can be seen in verse 7, "Deposuit," of the setting of odd-numbered verses in tone 2, verses 1, 7 and 11 of which are given in Example 4, pages 49-55.

The section containing the Magnificat settings concludes with a four-part *Benedicamus Domino* intended for use at the conclusion of Vespers. Very short and concise, it is notated under the mensural sign O3 and perhaps paraphrases in its superius a chant melody peculiar to the Spanish tradition.

Marian Antiphons.   The next section of the 1613 print contains, logically enough, the four seasonal Marian antiphons sung after certain of the Office Hours. Three of these, *Alma Redemptoris Mater, Regina caeli* and *Salve Regina,* are set for four voices, but *Ave Regina* is for five. None has a canonically derived part and each paraphrases, primarily in the superius, the chant melody to which it traditionally was sung monophonically. In only two of the antiphons, however, is the paraphrased chant the same as that to be found in modern liturgical books since both *Ave Regina* and *Regina caeli* utilize chants peculiar to the Spanish tradition. Also in keeping with Spanish practice is the alternatim treatment of *Salve Regina;* only the versicles "Vita dulcedo," "Ad te suspiramus," "Et Jesum" and "O clemens" receive a polyphonic setting, leaving the others either to be sung in chant or paraphrased instrumentally.

Miscellaneous Items.   The fifth section of the volume also is a small one and contains only five items, two for use in Office Hours and three for use in connection with the Mass. The first of these is an alternatim setting of *Te Deum laudamus,* which is sung after the last lesson of Matins on principal feasts. It, too, paraphrases a chant melody—the simpler one—to which this text traditionally was sung. The other Office item is the canticle of Zachary, *Benedictus,* sung daily at Lauds. All of the even-numbered verses of this canticle are set in tone 8 in a manner more closely resembling that used for the psalms which opened the volume than that found in the Magnificat settings. Undoubtedly the reason for the simple treatment accorded this canticle is the fact that Lauds usually was celebrated with much less musical solemnity than Vespers and this item was the only one in Lauds that was sung polyphonically with any frequency.

The first of the items for use in connection with the Mass liturgy is a setting of *Vidi aquam.* Again, the chant melody traditionally used with this text serves as the basis for the polyphonic setting, sometimes being loosely paraphrased and at other times supplying motival material for points of imitation. The traditional performance practice scheme of the item is, of course, reflected in the polyphonic setting. That is to say, the intonation of the antiphon and the first half of both the psalm verse and the doxology, performed by the cantors in a chant performance, are sung according to the original chant melody and here are assigned to the tenor voice, and that portion of the item which would have been sung by the entire chant choir is set polyphonically.

The setting of *Asperges me* which follows *Vidi aquam* is identical with the setting of this text with which Esquivel opened his 1608 collection of masses and is the only item in the 1613 volume which also appears in either of his two earlier publications. It, too, utilizes the chant traditionally associated with the text, but here this melody appears paraphrased in its entirety in the superius and those portions of the text which are sung monophonically according to the original chant are assigned to the superius rather than to the tenor.

The final item of this section is a motet. Described in the index and at the head of the page on which it begins as *Motetum commune ad omnia festa,* it was intended for use on the feast of any saint. Its versatility resulted from the generic nature of the text, which became specific only through the insertion of the name of whichever saint it was on whose feast the motet was sung: "O sancte N[omen], lumen aureum, Domini gratia servorum gemitus solita suscipe clementia." The setting, which extends to just less than fifty measures in transcription, probably enjoyed frequent use in the cathedral in Ciudad Rodrigo on the feasts of saints of lesser importance in the yearly liturgical cycle or whenever limited musical resources made it impractical to perform one of the items for four, five, six or eight voices in Esquivel's motet collection of 1608.

TABLE III

MAGNIFICAT SETTINGS WITH ODD-NUMBERED VERSES

TONE	NO. OF VOICES	VERSE 1	VERSE 3	VERSE 5	VERSE 7	VERSE 9	VERSE 11
1	5	SSATB	SSATB	SSAT	SSATB	SSATB	SSAATB Altus I: *Altus secundus in secunda.*
2	4	SATB	SATB	SATB	ATB	SATB	SSAATTBB Superius I: *Altus secundus in sub Diatessaron retro canit.* Altus I: *Tenor secundus in sub Diatessaron.*
3	4	SATB	SATB	AAB	SATB	SATB	SSAT
4	4	SATB	SSATB	SAT	SSAATB Altus I: *Superius secundus in Diatessaron.*	SATB	SSATB Bassus: *Tenor in Diatessaron.*
5	6	SSAATB	SSAATB	SAT	SSAATB	SSAATB	SSAATTB *Super octo tonos.* (The *Euouae* formulas of the eight tones, with the text "Saeculorum. Amen," are used as the first eight of the ten phrases of the Altus I.) Altus II: *Tenor primus in Diapason*
6	4	SATB	SATB	SSA	SATB	SATB	SSATTB Superius I: *Trinitas in unitate.* Superius II: *quod ascendit descendit in sexta.* Tenor II: *in sub Diapente.*
7	4	SATB	SATB	SSATB	SSAB	SATB	SATTB Altus: *Tenor secundus in sub Diatessaron, semibrevia tantum.*
8	4	SATB	SATB	SAB	SSATB	SSAATB Superius I: *Superius secundus in Diatessaron.*	SSAATTB Superius II: *Altus primus in sub Diapente* SSAATTBB Superius II: *Altus primus in secunda.* Altus II: *Superius primus in Diatessaron.* Tenor I: *Bassus secundus in sub Diapente.* Bassus I: *Tenor secundus in Diapason, semibrevia, et eorum pausas tantum.*

sections or of the "Sanctus" and "Pleni" sections, all set in one continuous unit. Only in a *Missa pro defunctis* did the complete Sanctus text normally continue to receive a polyphonic setting.[21]

The first of the mass ordinaries in the 1613 print is the *Missa Tu es Petrus*. It is written for five voices—SSATB—and is based on the Office antiphon *Tu es Petrus,* which is sung on the feasts of Saints Peter and Paul. From the fact, however, that Esquivel borrowed for use in this mass only the opening phrase of this antiphon, that is to say, only those notes to which the words "Tu es Petrus" are sung, and that he placed the mass at the head of the collection, it is evident that he viewed it primarily not as a special mass for use on the feast of Saints Peter and Paul but rather as a dedication to and a public acknowledgement of his patron, Pedro Ponce de León, who is addressed with the words "Tu es Petrus" in those sections in which the borrowed material is used as an ostinato.

Esquivel uses the opening phrase of the antiphon in one manner or another in each of the five movements. As a motive that can be modified and developed freely it appears not only at the beginning of the Kyrie, the Gloria, the Credo and the "Hosanna" of the Sanctus but also internally. The frequency with which the borrowed phrase appears in these items varies considerably, however, from one item to another and from section to section within the items. In the Kyrie, given as Example 5, page 56, the motive appears at least once in each part in "Kyrie I" and "Christe" and is so disposed that it is sounded essentially throughout both of these sections. In "Kyrie II," however, it occurs only in the second superius, the altus and the tenor, and is not heard at all during the last six of the fifteen measures of this section.

In the Gloria the motive is used with much less frequency than in the Kyrie and only two of the voices rather than all five have the motive at the beginning. In fact, the motive appears but nine times in the entire "Et in terra" and only thirteen in the "Qui tollis." Perhaps Esquivel thought it unnecessary to use it with any greater frequency here since he had so definitively established in the Kyrie just what musical motive it was on which he had based this mass.

Perhaps it is for this same reason that the motive appears with even less frequency in the Credo than in the Gloria, proportionately speaking. Here each of the four sections of the Credo opens with the motive appearing in two of the voices, but aside from these eight statements it is heard no more than twenty other times during the course of the entire movement and then often in an internal voice where it hardly is audible to the listener.

---

[21] The Sanctus settings in masses by earlier composers such as Guerrero and his contemporaries which remained in the repertory throughout the seventeenth century and beyond were shortened by various means. In those settings in which the "Sanctus" portion of the text was set independently of the "Pleni" section, this usually was accomplished by redisposing the text so that not only the "Sanctus" but also the "Pleni" and sometimes even the "Hosanna" textual sections were all sung to the music which originally had served only for the "Sanctus" section and sometimes also by omitting the "Benedictus" and "Hosanna II" entirely. As for those settings in which the "Sanctus" and the "Pleni" sections of the text were set in one continuous musical unit, the shortening most often was achieved simply by omitting all other sections. Both of these methods also were used to shorten the long tripartite Agnus Dei settings in the masses of the same composers. Particularly instructive in this matter is the copy of Guerrero's *Missarum liber secundus* of 1582 which is preserved in the archives of the cathedral of Malaga. In this copy (which lacks the title page and the opening six-voiced *Missa Surge, propera* and is not listed in RISM A/I) the Sanctus of every mass but one has been shortened by means of a redisposition of text. Three of the Agnus Dei settings have been similarly modified so that the music which originally served for only the first invocation sufficed for the entire text of the Agnus Dei.

In the Sanctus and the Agnus Dei the motive is once more fully in view, so to speak.   In the "Hosanna" it is used motivally in each voice and with such frequency that it is continually sounded in one voice or another beginning at one or another of the following three pitch levels and their upper octaves: d', g' and c'. It also is heard throughout the "Sanctus-Pleni" section in the form of an ostinato in the tenor, which sings the motive with its original text four times, beginning alternately on g' and d'. It is heard in none of the other voices, however, except the superius, where it appears once as the initial phrase of this part and thus anticipates the slightly later first statement of the motive as an ostinato in the tenor. See Example 6, pages 57-60, which contains the entire Sanctus since the "Benedictus" was not composed by Esquivel.

In the first of the two Agnus Dei invocations the motive, again with its original text, again appears as an ostinato, but this time it is assigned to the second superius and is heard six times beginning alternately on g' and d''. And, as in the Sanctus, the only appearance of the motive here other than in its manifestation as an ostinato is at the beginning of the superius, where it appears in anticipation of its appearance in the superius secundus. In the second invocation of the Agnus Dei, in which the number of parts is increased to six by the addition of an altus secundus, the motive once more is used with its original text to form an ostinato, this time in two voices. It is notated in the superius, which sings it four times, beginning it alternately on g' and d'', and from this part the tenor is derived by means of the canonic inscription *In Sub Diapente*. As a result, the motive is heard four more times beginning alternately on c' and g' one breve later than in the superius. The canon which produces the tenor is but one of the two to be found in this section, however, since the superius secundus is derived from the altus primus by singing that part *in diatessaron* at the distance of two breves. Esquivel thus fittingly concluded this dedicatory mass by simultaneously proclaiming the name of his distinguished patron and exercising his contrapuntal skills in his honor.[22]

The *Missa quarti toni,* set for the same five voices as the *Missa Tu es Petrus,* contains a number of features which place it somewhat apart from other late Renaissance mass ordinaries. For one thing, two of its movements, the Gloria and Credo, paraphrase a corresponding chant melody in their superius primus parts whereas the three other movements seem to contain no pre-existent material of any kind. Also, despite the title, one of the movements, the Credo, is not in the fourth mode at all but rather in the first. Furthermore, the Gloria and Credo contain stylistic features which set them apart not only from the three other movements but from each other as well and one cannot help but wonder if these two movements were composed not only considerably before the others but also independently of one another. Finally, certain of the movements are of a disproportionate length.

The Kyrie of the *Missa quarti toni,* which extends to forty-three measures in transcription, is by far the longest of those included in this collection although it is slightly exceeded in length by two in Esquivel's first publication, namely those of the *Missa Ductus est Jesus* and the *Missa Gloriose confessor*

---

[22] Equivel's *Missa Tu es Petrus* has so many features in common with Morales's *Missa Tu es vas electionis* that it is difficult to escape the conclusion that he used the earlier composer's mass as a model. Morales's mass also was dedicatory in nature and opened his *Missarum liber secundus,* which was published in Rome in 1544 and dedicated to Pope Paul III. The pre-existent material on which Morales based his mass also consisted of but a single phrase of music sung to a text containing the name of the dedicatee–"Tu es vas electionis, Sanctissime Paule"–and was utilized in the same manner as the opening phrase of the antiphon *Tu es Petrus* in Esquivel's mass: sometimes as a cantus firmus or as an ostinato sung with its original text and sometimes as a source for motival material which could be treated imitatively when the composer so desired.

Domini. Each of the three sections has its own distinctive motival material, most of which reflects the general melodic characteristics of plainsong items in mode 4. In their specific form, however, the motives all seem to be creations of Esquivel. (That the first six pitches of the opening motive of the Kyrie are identical with the first six notes of the sequence *Lauda Sion,* in mode 7, undoubtedly is fortuitous.) Harmonic elements also place the Kyrie firmly in the fourth mode, particularly the final harmonic constructs of each of the three sections, the first of which concludes with a construct built on *e,* the second with one on *A* and the third with one again on *e.* See Example 7 for the opening section of this item, pages 61-62.

The Gloria, the beginning of which is given in Example 8, page 63, can best be described as a harmonization of the very simple chant Gloria which forms part of Mass XV in the *Graduale Romanum.* The chant, only slightly modified, appears in the superius primus throughout the movement; the other voices, which often declaim the text simultaneously with the superius primus, merely support it harmonically. The result is an extremely concise setting which, as mentioned above, stylistically contrasts rather sharply with the other movements of the mass, including the Credo, which also paraphrases a pre-existent chant melody in its superius primus. Neither in the Gloria nor in the Credo, however, is the pre-existent chant as audible to the listener as one might expect since in both movements the fifth voice part, the superius secundus, almost always moves above rather than below the chant-bearing superius primus.[23]

In the Credo the pre-eixtent chant in the superius primus is that which appears in the *Graduale Romanum* as Credo IV. In its original form this chant is in mode 1 and since all of its modal characteristics were retained by Esquivel when he adapted it for use in this movement, the polyphonic setting of it also is in mode 1, as can be seen in Example 9, page 64. Why Esquivel chose to include in a *Missa quarti toni* a Credo based on a chant in mode 1 rather than one based on a chant in mode 4, such as Credo I or Credo II of the *Graduale,* is puzzling and one can only conjecture as to why he did this. Perhaps, as we suggested above, Esquivel composed both the Credo and the Gloria of this mass independently of each other at some earlier time and then, when preparing his second book of masses, added to them the three other movements, all of which he cast in the mode of the Gloria rather than in that of the Credo, in order to add another mass to the collection with as little effort as possible.

As was seen in Table IV, the Sanctus of the *Missa quarti toni* is one of two settings of this item in Esquivel's second book of masses which consists of only the first section of the text. Extending to only eighteen measures in length in transcription, it seems to contain no pre-existent material and definitely is written in the fourth mode.

The text of the Agnus Dei also is shortened and consists of but one invocation which concludes with the words "miserere nobis." It thus stands apart from the other Agnus Dei settings in this collection since these all have two invocations, the second of which always concludes with "dona nobis pacem," has one additional voice and at least one canonically derived part. (In the first book of masses, two of the Agnus Dei settings, those of the *Missa hexachordum* and the *Missa Gloriose confessor Domini,* consisted of but a single invocation.) The single invocation constituting the Agnus Dei of the *Missa quarti toni* is, however, of longer than average length and is surpassed in this respect only by the extremely long first invocation of the Agnus Dei of the *Missa Tu es Petrus.* Again, no pre-existent material seems to be used and the mode definitely is the fourth.

---

[23] In the music of Esquivel, as in that of many Spanish composers of the later Renaissance, a superius secundus often occupies a higher range than does a superius primus. Similarly, a bassus secundus usually moves above a bassus primus.

The four-part *Missa de Beata Virgine in Sabbato* or *Missa B. Mariae in Sabbato*, as it is designated in the index, is the shortest of Esquivel's masses and was, as its title indicates, intended for use at the Marian votive Mass usually celebrated on every Saturday in addition to the feast called for by the liturgical calendar. It contains no Credo because this item was not used in a votive Mass and, as was customary, each of the other four items utilizes to some extent musical material taken from the corresponding ordinary chant traditionally sung at these Marian votive services. Except in the Gloria, however, a limited amount of chant material is used. In the Kyrie, which draws on the Kyrie of Mass IX in the *Graduale*, both the superius and tenor of "Kyrie I" begin with a motive constructed from the first four pitches of the first of the chant "Kyrie I" invocations and then continue freely, whereas the altus and the bassus contain no borrowed material at all. A greater portion of the "Christe" is structured from borrowed material. Here the first phrase of each of the four voices consists of a motive based on the first five notes of the first of the chant "Christe" invocations. The second of the two phrases of the tenor and of the bassus also consist of the same material, as does the third of the three phrases of the superius. Only the second of the superius phrases and the second and third of the altus phrases contain no borrowed material. For some reason "Kyrie II" does not, as one might expect, draw on the first of the last three chant "Kyrie" invocations for its motival material. Rather, it borrows from the very first invocation, just as did "Kyrie I," and both the superius and the bassus open with a motive almost identical with that with which the superius and the tenor of "Kyrie I" began. And, as in "Kyrie I," no additional chant material is used. See Example 10, pages 65-66.

The Gloria is based on the chant Gloria which also occurs in Mass IX of the *Graduale*. Here, however, the entire chant melody is utilized in the superius in a modernized form in much the same way as were the melodies of the Gloria of Mass XV and Credo IV in the superius primus of the Gloria and Credo of the *Missa quarti toni*. Also, motival material in the other voices frequently is derived either from the original form of the chant or from the form in which it is presented in the top voice and the underlaying of the text often deviates somewhat from that of the present-day form of the chant, as can be seen in Example 11, page 67, which presents the beginning of the Gloria.

Once again the Sanctus appears in a truncated form and in this mass, as in the *Missa quarti toni*, it consists only of the first section of the text. The chant melody which appears in a modernized form in part of the superius and motivally in other voices is that which is included in Mass XVII of the *Graduale* but which in the Spanish tradition was associated with Marian votive Masses.

The Agnus Dei has the usual two invocations and each contains motival elements and reminiscences, particularly in the upper voice, of the chant Agnus Dei of Mass XVII, also associated with Marian votive Masses in Spain. Neither invocation, however, employs the chant in the superius in the full fashion in which it occurs in the Gloria. The second invocation is for five voices, the added one being a superius secundus from which the bassus is derived canonically according to the prescription *Qui se humiliat exaltabitur. Duodecim.* This produces a bassus which is an inversion of the superius secundus and results in a mirror canon, the beginning of which is given in Example 12, page 68. This specific example of a mirror canon is a very simple one because the melodic line of the superius secundus is limited to a fifth, f' to c'', and whenever f' occurs in the upper of the two voices, and consequently c' appears in the lower and an interval of a fourth is produced, the tenor moves below the bassus and becomes the lowest-sounding voice, singing f or a.

Immediately following the *Missa de Beata Virgine in Sabbato* there occurs on pages 466-69 a three-part Marian motet, *Surge, propera, amica mea.* That this also was intended for use at Marian votive Masses is evident from the inscription at the top of page 468 (which undoubtedly also was at the top of page 466 before the book was trimmed when last bound): *Motetum Beatae Mariae cantandum in organo.* Because this item is listed in the index immediately following the *Missa de Beata Virgine in Sabbato* but without any indication that it is a motet, all who have commented on this print of Esquivel have assumed that it contained a three-part *Missa Surge, propera.* That this is not the case would have been evident from the index, which indicates that the item occupies only four pages, hardly enough for a mass ordinary, had Pedrell included the page numbers in the entry on Esquivel in his *Diccionario.*

The four-voiced *Missa Hoc est praeceptum meum* is, as was the *Missa Tu es Petrus,* based on an Office antiphon, in this case the first antiphon sung at First Vespers on feasts of apostles and evangelists occurring outside of paschaltide. The manner in which Esquivel utilizes the pre-existent material is similar in the two masses but here he makes use of the entire antiphon, which is in the eighth mode, rather than just the opening phrase. Thus, he sometimes derives from the three phrases of the antiphon motives to be used imitatively and at other times he presents the antiphon either in whole or in part as a cantus firmus.

Both a motival and a quasi-cantus firmus treatment of the antiphon serve as the structural bases of the Kyrie. In "Kyrie I" every phrase but one—the third of the altus—begins with motival material derived from the opening phrase of the antiphon. In the "Christe" the first three voices to enter, the altus, tenor and bassus, all open with an imitatively treated motive, the beginning of which is derived from the second phrase of the antiphon, "ut diligatis invicem," whereas the last voice to enter, the superius, presents in cantus firmus fashion the opening phrase of the antiphon. Surprisingly, it begins on an *f* rather than a *c.* Much the same approach is used in "Kyrie II" since, again, the last voice to enter, the altus, presents the opening phrase of the antiphon in cantus firmus manner and the three other voices either contain motival material derived from the same phrase or are freely composed. Here the cantus firmus-like presentation of the phrase begins on a *g* rather than a *c* but lacks the sharp necessary to produce an exact transposition. See Example 13, pages 69-70, which presents the entire Kyrie.

The Gloria, cast in the usual bipartite form, utilizes the antiphon with its original text as a cantus firmus in both sections. In the "Et in terra," which is the only section of a mass by Esquivel notated under the sign $\emptyset$, it appears in the altus, as can be seen in Example 14, page 71, which consists of the beginning of the Gloria. Here the notational level at which the antiphon appears is the same as that at which it occurs in chant sources and the last phrase is repeated once in order to achieve the length necessary for the section. In the "Qui tollis," however, the antiphon appears in the tenor without any phrase being repeated and, as in "Kyrie II," it is notated a fifth higher and without the sharp needed to produce an exact transposition. In both sections the three other voices are devoid of material derived from the antiphon; Esquivel undoubtedly felt that the presence of the antiphon as a cantus firmus was sufficient.

In the Credo not only is there no cantus firmus but only a minimal amount of motival material is derived from the antiphon. The "Patrem" begins with an imitatively treated motive based on the first phrase of the antiphon and consequently is reminiscent of the beginning of the Kyrie but after the first few measures it continues in an essentially free manner. The brief "Et incarnatus," however, given in Example 15, page 72, makes some use of motives derived from all three phrases of the antiphon after beginning with freely-composed material, as does the "Crucifixus," but the longer "Et in Spiritum" contains only the slightest references to the antiphon. Thus, this Credo, like that of the *Missa Tu es Petrus,* is largely freely composed in the sense that only a minimal amount of the melodic material of the various voices is derived from the antiphon on which the mass as a whole is based.

Esquivel again resorted to cantus firmus treatment of the antiphon in the "Sanctus-Pleni" section of the Sanctus. The entire antiphon with its original text appears in the tenor and, as in "Kyrie II" and "Qui tollis," it again is notated a fifth higher than it appears in chant sources and again without benefit of the sharp necessary for an exact transposition. Esquivel provided no setting of the "Hosanna" and in the "Benedictus," set for SSAT rather than SATB, he used melodic material which only occasionally makes the most tenuous of references to the antiphon.

The Agnus Dei consists of the customary two invocations, the first of which is free from references to the antiphon except for the imitatively treated motive which appears with the words "qui tollis peccata mundi" in three of the voices. The second invocation, however, which is set for SSATB and has its tenor derived from the altus by means of the canon *in Subdiatessaron,* again presents the antiphon as a cantus firmus with its own text. And, again, it appears a fifth higher than in chant sources, without the needed sharp. See Example 16, pages 73-74, which consists of the second of the two invocations.

Both of the other masses in the 1613 print are based on motets. For the first of these, the four-voiced *Missa Quasi cedrus,* Esquivel borrowed motival material from Guerrero's bipartite motet *Quasi cedrus,* for the feast of the Assumption, which had appeared in that composer's first publication, the collection of motets from 1555 entitled *Sacrae cantiones.*[24] In reworking the material he borrowed from this motet Esquivel employed the conventional techniques of his time but deviated from the accepted practice of assigning the same motival material to the same structural places in the various items such as the beginning of each of the movements and at the beginning of the various sections of these. For example, the opening material of the motet, sung to the words "Quasi cedrus exaltata sum," given in Example 17, page 75, serves as the source of the material for the first section of the Kyrie, Example 18, page 76, and plays a somewhat lesser role at the beginning of the Gloria, Example 19, page 77. It is, however, material from the beginning of the secunda pars, sung to the words "Tota pulchra es, amica mea," Example 20, page 78, which is used for the beginning of the Credo, Example 21, page 79, and the beginning of the Sanctus, Example 22, page 80. The beginning of the Agnus Dei, Example 23, page 81, however, is constructed from material which in the motet occurs toward the end of the secunda pars with the words "veni, sponsa mea" and "veni, coronaberis."

Because all five items do not begin with the same motival material one of the characteristic features of the cyclic parody mass—indeed, the very element which makes the cyclic nature of the work immediately evident—is missing from the *Missa Quasi cedrus* and consequently it can be identified as a cyclic mass only by reference to the motet on which it is based. It is not yet possible to state whether the use of different motives at the beginnings of different items is primarily an idiosyncrasy of Esquivel or whether it is symptomatic of the end of the Spanish parody mass tradition because far too few of these late masses have been studied. It should be noted, however, that in one of the parody masses in Esquivel's earlier collection from 1608, *Missa Ave, Virgo sanctissima,* the Sanctus begins with material different from that with which

---

[24] *RISM* A/1 attributes to Guerrero an earlier collection of motets from 1547, assigning it the number G 4866. Actually, the four part books so listed are all exemplars of the motet collection from 1597, G 4877. Thus, the collection from 1555, *Sacrae cantiones,* G 4867, is still the earliest known publication by this composer. It should be noted that the four part books listed as G 4866, all of which are preserved at the Instituto Español de Musicología in Barcelona, include one copy of the superius, not two, two copies of the altus, not one, and one copy of the bassus. The superius and bassus books and one copy of the altus formerly were owned by José Subirá. The other copy of the altus has a manuscript appendix containing several items, almost all of which are by Guerrero.

the four other items open.[25] In all other aspects the *Missa Quasi cedrus* conforms to the conventions of the time. The Gloria is cast in the usual two sections, the Credo in the usual four, the Sanctus is shortened, and the second Agnus Dei invocation is set for five voices, the fifth of which is an altus secundus derived from the altus primus by means of the canon *In secuda*.

The other parody mass and the last of the ordinaries in the 1613 print is the four-part *Missa Hortus conclusus*. It is based on material from what must have been one of the most popular of the Marian motets of Rodrigo de Ceballos if one can take as an indication of popularity the fact that it is preserved in at least four extant manuscripts and also was to be found in an incomplete set of part books, now lost, which at the end of the last century was in the private library of the famous Spanish composer and violinist, Jesús de Monasterio.[26] This motet also is bipartite and Esquivel again extracted material from the secunda pars, "Veni, sponsa mea," as well as from the prima pars. In this mass, however, Esquivel observed the convention of beginning all five movements with motival material drawn from the opening of the motet, which is given in Example 24, page 82. Nevertheless, only in the Kyrie do all four of the voices begin with a motive structured from this material. In the Gloria and Agnus Dei only three open with similarly derived material and in the Credo and Sanctus only two voices begin in this fashion. Interestingly, in the second of the two Agnus Dei invocations, which is *a 5*, the altus primus and the altus secundus (the latter of which is derived canonically from the former) also open with a motive based on the same material. In order to see how Esquivel tended to treat his borrowed material here, see Examples 25 and 26, pages 83-85, which present, respectively, the opening measures of the Kyrie and the Sanctus.

Following the *Missa Hortus conclusus* and concluding this section is a setting of *Deo gratias*, the response to the versicle *Ite, missa est,* for use at the conclusion of Mass. Here, again, because Pedrell did not give page numbers when he printed the index of the print in his *Diccionario*, all who have commented on the contents of the book have erroneously assumed, as they also did in the case of the motet *Surge, propera, amica mea,* that this item was another mass ordinary. Again, such an assumption would not have been possible had the numbers been printed because this piece, like the motet, occupies far too few pages, in this instance only two, 560-61, to have been a mass ordinary. The setting, *a 4*, is typically brief—it extends only to seven measures in transcription—and has in its superius reminiscences of the *Ite, missa est-Deo gratias* chant based on Kyrie IV of the *Graduale Romanum*.

---

[25] A similar situation prevails in certain of Victoria's parody masses; see, for example, his *Missa O quam gloriosa*. It is well-known that Pedro Cerone stated in his *El Melopeo y maestro* of 1613 that the beginning of each movement of a parody mass should be based on the same material: "Mas en el componer una Missa, por fuerça y de obligacion (servando su verdadera orden) *conviene que la Invencion en el principio del primero Kyrie, y en el de la Gloria in excelsis Deo, del Credo, del Sanctus, y en el del primero Agnus Dei, sea una misma: digo que ha de ser una mesma cosa en la invencion,* y no en las Consonancias y accompanamiento." (*Libro* XII, *Cap.* XIII; p. 687, lines 11 *ff.*) This prescription should not, however, necessarily be taken as indicative that this was the only practice of Spanish composers during the first decades of the seventeenth century because Cerone seems to have based his discussion of the principles of parody mass composition more on remarks made by Pietro Ponzio in his *Ragionamento* of 1588 than on what composers themselves were doing at the time he was writing—or perhaps better, compiling—his treatise. See Lewis Lockwood, "On 'Parody' as Term and Concept in 16th-Century Music," *Aspects of Medieval and Renaissance Music,* ed. Jan La Rue et al. (New York: W. W. Norton, 1966), pp. 560-75.

[26] Granada, Capilla Real, Archivo capitular, Ms. 3, 39*v*-44*r*; Seville, Catedral, Archivo capitular, Ms. 1, 87*v*-91*r*; Toledo, Catedral, Biblioteca capitular, Ms. 7, 9*v*-13*r*; Valladolid, Parroquia de Santiago, Archivo, Ms. s. n. (= Diego Sánchez codex), 54*v*-56*r*. For information concerning the part books once owned by Monasterio, see the entry "Ceballos (Rodrigo de)" in Pedrell's *Diccionario*. For information concerning Monasterio, see José Subirá, "Epistolario de F. A. Gevaert y J. de Monasterio," *Anuario Musical* 16 (1961), 217-46.

Items for the Mass and Office of the Dead. The items *pro defunctis* with which the volume concludes are, in the order of their appearance in the print, a setting *a 4* of *Responde mihi,* a lesson from Matins; a four-part *Missa pro defunctis;* a four-part setting of the final three versicles of the *Dies irae;* a setting *a 5* of *Ne recorderis,* a responsory from Matins; and a setting *a 4* and *a 5,* respectively, of the versicle *Requiescant in pace* and the response *Amen.* Why the two items for use in Matins, *Responde mihi* and *Ne recorderis,* are separated by the mass is not clear; perhaps this was a mistake on the part of the printer.

As was mentioned earlier, Esquivel also concluded his first book of masses with items *pro defunctis,* in that case a mass for five voices and the six-voiced setting of *In paradisum,* which also appeared in the 1608 motet collection. By including another *Missa pro defunctis* in his 1613 collection Esquivel followed the example of at least two illustrious predecessors who also composed two masses *pro defunctis.* One can only conjecture why some Spanish composers wrote two of these masses. Perhaps one of them was intended for use in the many votive Masses *pro defunctis* that were celebrated at that time and the other was for use at funerals. Such a conjecture is supported in Esquivel's case by the fact that his *Missa pro defunctis* for five voices appeared in company with his setting of the ceremonial antiphon *In paradisum,* which is for the burial service, whereas the mass for four voices was accompanied by a lesson and a responsory from the second nocturn of Matins for the dead. That he set texts from the second nocturn of this Office Hour rather than from the first is proof that, at least in the case of the items for Matins, Esquivel, in his 1613 print, was providing music for a votive celebration of the liturgy for the dead rather than for a celebration on a day of burial, that is, an actual funeral service. This is evident from the rubrics of the breviary of Clement VIII, which prescribed that on the day of burial either all three nocturns of Matins were to be said or only the first, whereas for votive celebrations the first nocturn was to be used on Sunday, Monday and Thursday, the second on Tuesday and Friday, and the third on Wednesday and Saturday. Thus, it is not improbable that all of the items *pro defunctis* in the 1613 print were intended to be sung at a weekly votive celebration of the liturgy for the dead that probably occurred every Friday and that those in the 1608 book of masses were for use at actual funeral services.

In composing the two items for Matins Esquivel again followed the Spanish conventions of his time. His setting of *Responde mihi,* the first lesson of the second nocturn of Matins for the dead, is written in a simple quasi-chordal manner reflecting the essential features of a lesson tone and thus allows the text to be fully understood by the listener. In the responsory *Ne recorderis,* which follows the third and last lesson of the second nocturn, he polyphonically set only those portions of the text which in Spanish practice normally received such treatment and incorporated into the superius part the chant to which these portions traditionally were sung monophonically. The form of the responsories used after the lessons in Matins for the dead is the one used for all greater responsories of Matins. That is to say, it consists of a respond which in the chant tradition was sung by the entire schola (except, of course, for the functional intonation sung by a soloist) and which was followed by a soloistically performed verse, after which the latter portion of the respond was repeated by the schola. A second soloistically performed verse, consisting of the words "Gloria Patri, et Filio, et Spiritui Sancto" or, in the case of Matins for the dead, of the words "Requiem aeternam dona eis, Domine, et lux perpetua luceat eis," was added to the third and last responsory of each nocturn, after which the schola again repeated the latter portion of the respond. Thus, the full text and original formal scheme of the responsory *Ne recorderis* is as follows.

SCHOLA: *Respond.* Ne recorderis peccata mea, Domine, dum veneris judicare saeculum per ignem.

SOLOIST: *Verse.* Dirige, Domine Deus meus, in conspectu tuo viam meam

SCHOLA:	*Respond.*	dum veneris judicare saeculum per ignem.
SOLOIST:	*Verse.*	Requiem aeternam dona eis, Domine, et lux perpetua luceat eis
SCHOLA:	*Respond.*	dum veneris judicare saeculum per ignem.

When composing a greater responsory for Matins of any occasion the general Renaissance practice was to provide a polyphonic setting of that portion of the text sung by the schola and to leave those portions which in the chant tradition were performed soloistically to be sung according to the original chant. Thus, in the case of *Ne recorderis,* for example, the entire respond except perhaps for the words "Ne recorderis," which served as the soloistically performed intonation, normally received polyphonic treatment and the verse or verses were left to be sung according to their original chant melody.

Spanish composers usually followed the same practice when composing responsories for Matins of greater feasts such as Christmas and Easter. When composing the responsories used in Matins for the dead, however, the Spanish composer normally followed a decidedly different pattern in applying polyphony to the text. Instead of following the otherwise universal Renaissance practice of polyphonically setting those portions which in the chant tradition were performed by the schola, he set only the initial words of each section of the text. Thus, Esquivel's setting of *Ne recorderis* consists of polyphony only for the words "Ne recorderis," "dum veneris," "Dirige" and, again, "dum veneris;" the remaining portions of the text are left to be sung according to their original chant melody. It should be noted, incidentally, that here, as in most other settings, the initial words of that portion of the respond which is repeated after the verse— "dum veneris" in this instance—receive a different musical setting for their second statement. Sometimes the Spanish composer also supplied music for the initial words of the second verse—"Requiem aeternam dona eis, Domine"—and still another setting of the initial words needed for the final repeat of the latter portion of the respond with which the third responsory of a nocturn concluded. Esquivel chose not to do this but he did append, as was customary, a setting of the three versicles—Kyrie eleison, Christe eleison, Kyrie eleison—which followed the responsory.

The origin of this unusual Spanish manner of applying polyphony to the greater responsories of Matins for the dead, a manner which obscures, even contradicts, the formal scheme of the text, has not yet been investigated. Perhaps it derives from a medieval Spanish chant tradition in which each phrase of these responsories was intoned by the cantor and from the medieval practice of applying polyphony to the soloistically performed portions of a responsorial item rather than to those portions which were sung by the schola.

The *Missa pro defunctis* of the 1613 print consists of the same items as does that of the 1608 print—introit, Kyrie, tract, offertory, Sanctus, Agnus Dei and communion—and, as did the earlier setting, it exhibits all of those features which distinguish most Spanish settings of these texts from those written by composers working in other areas of Europe. In each of the three ordinary items this feature consists of the specific chant melody which is incorporated into the superius part since in Spain each of these items traditionally was sung to a chant melody other than that used elsewhere. Thus, Esquivel's Kyrie is based on a chant unique to the peninsular tradition, his Sanctus utilizes the melody which appears with this text in Mass XV of the *Graduale* and his Agnus Dei has in its superius a variant form of the Agnus Dei of the same chant mass. It should be noted, however, that in the *Graduale* the musical form of this Agnus Dei is *ABA* whereas in the Spanish tradition the second and third invocations are interchanged, resulting in the form *AAB*, and that the material constituting the *B* section is slightly different in certain places.

In the introit and offertory the distinctively Spanish characteristic is the length of the intonation and hence the point at which polyphony begins. Elsewhere in Europe the intonation of the introit consisted of the word "Requiem" and polyphony began at "aeternam"; in the offertory it usually extended through "Domine Jesu Christe" and polyphony began at "Rex gloriae." In Spain, however, both intonations usually were longer and consisted of "Requiem aeternam" and "Domine Jesu Christe, Rex gloriae," respectively.. Thus, in Spanish settings of the introit polyphony normally begins at the words "dona eis" and in the offertory at "libera animas."

Other distinctive features frequently but not always found in Spanish masses *pro defunctis* include the omission of the offertory verse "Hostias" and the disregard of the psalmodic character of the verse of the communion, which results in this portion of the communion being set in the same manner as is the antiphon. Both of these features are present in Esquivel's setting in the 1613 print. A lack of interest in the *Dies irae,* which became an official part of the liturgy throughout Spain only when the missal of Pius V was introduced into the various dioceses, also was characteristic of the Spanish tradition. Undoubtedly, the reason for this was that the sentiments expressed in this Italian invention were alien to the Spanish mentality. Thus, Esquivel included nothing for this text in his 1608 print and in that of 1613 he provided, probably as an afterthought, music only for the last three versicles, "Lachrymosa," "Judicandus" and "Huic ergo," and the concluding "Amen." That there was no Spanish tradition governing the setting of this text is evident from two facts: only in this item did Esquivel make no use of the chant melody to which the text was sung and he disregarded the formal structure of the text by setting the three versicles in a single, continuous musical unit.

All of the movements except the offertory and the versicles from the *Dies irae,* the only two items which speak explicitly of the pains and horrors of damnation, express a profound serenity. As can be seen in Examples 27 and 28, pages 86-87, which present the beginning of the introit and of the Sanctus, they achieve this by melodic lines which, except for that of the bassus part, move in a predominantly step-wise manner; by a slow harmonic rhythm based almost exclusively on the use of harmonic constructs in what today would be called root position; and by limiting dissonances primarily to carefully prepared suspensions. How sharply the expressive quality of the *Dies irae* versicles (and of the offertory) differs from that of the other items and how this was achieved can be seen from a comparison of the beginning of the versicles, given in Example 29, page 88, with the beginning of the introit and of the Sanctus.

The volume concludes with a setting of the versicle *Requiescant in pace* and its response, *Amen.* Here also, as in the *Deo gratias* at the end of the mass ordinary settings, Esquivel incorporated into the superius the chant material associated with the text.

*   *   *

The discovery of a copy of the 1613 print approximately doubles the quantity of music by Esquivel that has been preserved and makes possible a definitive list of the works he presently is known to have published. Thus, his settings of official texts of the Mass liturgy include one *Asperges me* and one *Vidi aquam,* eleven mass ordinaries (not thirteen) and one *Deo gratias* response to *Ite, missa est.* For the liturgy for the dead there are two masses, a setting of part of the *Dies irae,* a *Requiescant in pace-Amen,* one setting of the ceremonial antiphon *In paradisum* (not two), the lesson *Responde mihi* and the responsory *Ne recorderis.* Items for Vespers include eight psalms, thirty hymns (not twenty-nine), sixteen Magnificat settings, a *Benedicamus Domino* and a setting of each of the four Marian antiphons. For Matins there is *Te Deum laudamus,* for Lauds a setting of the canticle

Benedictus, and for Compline a setting of the canticle *Nunc dimittis* and of the hymn *Te lucis ante terminum.* Finally, there are seventy-one motets for optional use in the Mass.

Whether these are all the works that Esquivel composed is, of course, uncertain. The fact that no music known to be by him other than some of the items appearing in one or another of the two prints from 1608 has yet been found in manuscript sources suggests that the list might well contain everything he wrote.[27] Nevertheless, the absence from the list of settings of any of the official texts of the liturgy of Palm Sunday and the final three days of Holy Week raises doubts and one wonders if he also published a volume of music for these occasions, no copy of which has survived. Perhaps this question will be answered by consulting the previously mentioned history of the cathedral of Ciudad Rodrigo by Antonio Sánchez Cabañas since, according to Mateo Hernández Vegas, at least some of the works of Esquivel are discussed there.[28]

A definitive evaluation of Esquivel's role in the historical development of Spanish music cannot be made, of course, until a substantial amount of his music and that of his contemporaries and immediate predecessors and successors has been made available in modern editions and intensively studied. Some tentative conclusions can, however, be drawn from the limited evidence presently available. This suggests that Esquivel, even though not all of his work was consistently of the highest quality, must be ranked as one of the foremost members of that generation of Spanish composers whose activity was centered in the first quarter of the seventeenth century.

His technical skills were considerable, as can be seen from his handling of the great variety of canonic devices utilized in the final verses of his Magnificat settings containing odd-numbered verses and in his reworking of the borrowed material on which he based his parody masses. His sensitivity to the Latin of his texts, although not that of a Guerrero or a Ceballos, usually enabled him to write highly distinctive and expressive melodic lines for the beginnings of the various phrases of a text, particularly in his motets, but it must be added that his extensions of these lines into accompanying "countersubjects" occasionally are somewhat less felicitous in their relationship to the text.

Perhaps the most interesting aspect of Esquivel's music from the standpoint of the historian is the conflict often to be found in it between its technical vocabulary and that which it seems to wish to express. The technical vocabulary is, of course, that of the late Renaissance but the expressive intent frequently seems to be that of an incipient Baroque spirit, particularly in a number of the motets. Esquivel's effort to solve this problem was limited to the introduction of a mild chromaticism similar to that to be found in the music of a number of Italian composers active some three or four decades earlier. The spirit of the place and age in which he worked made nothing else possible. It is to Esquivel's credit, however, that he seems to have sensed this new spirit, which was not to come to full fruition in Spanish music, more strongly than did most of his contemporaries.

───────────────

[27] See Appendix II, pp. 93-95.
[28] See Appendix III, pp. 97-98.

MUSIC EXAMPLES

Example 1. *Dixit Dominus Sexti toni*

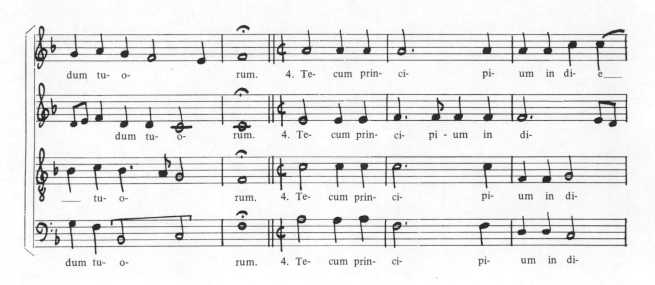

Example 1—2

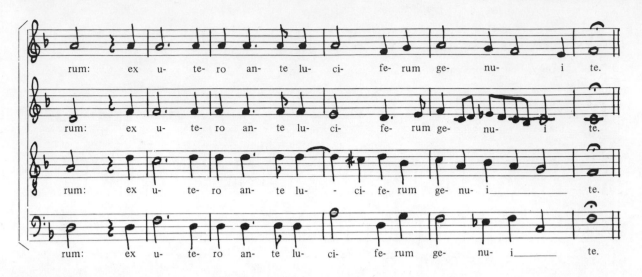

rum: ex u- te- ro an te lu- ci- fe- rum ge- nu- i te.

rum: ex u- te- ro an te lu- ci- fe- rum ge- nu- i te.

rum: ex u- te- ro an te lu- ci- fe- rum ge- nu- i_____ te.

rum: ex u- te- ro an te lu- ci- fe- rum ge- nu- i_____ te.

6. Do- mi- nus a de- -xtris tu- - is,

6. Do- mi- nus a de- -xtris_____ tu- is,

6. Do- mi- nus a_____ de- xtris tu- - is,_____

6. Do- mi- nus a de- -xtris tu- - is,

con- fre- git in di- - e i- rae su- ae re- ges.

con- fre- git in di e i- rae_____ su- ae re- ges.

con- fre- git in di e i- -rae su- ae_____ re- ges.

con- fre- git in di e i- rae su- ae re- ges.

40

Example 1—3

Example 1–4

Example 2. *Veni Creator Spiritus*

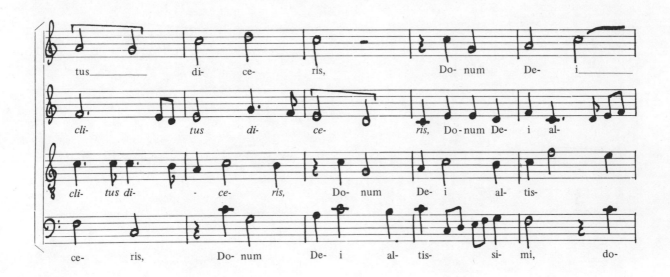

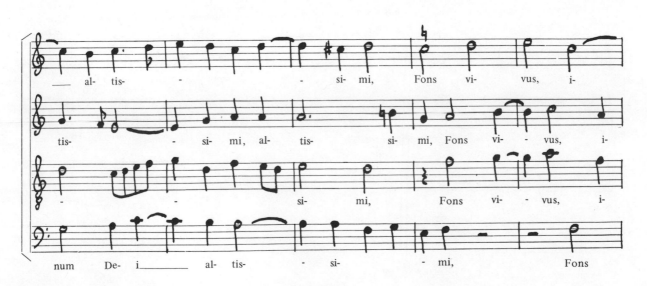

Example 2−2

-gnis, ca- - ri-tas, ca- - ri-tas,_____

gnis,_____ ca- ri-tas, *fons vi- vus, i-* gnis, ca- - ri- - tas,

gnis, ca- ri-tas, *fons vi- vus, i-* gnis, ca- - ri- tas,

vi- vus, i- gnis,_____ ca- - ri- - tas,

_____ Et_____ spi- ri- - ta- - - lis

Et_____ spi- ri- ta- lis un- cti- - o, un-

Et_____ spi- ri- ta- lis un- - - -

Et spi- ri- ta- lis, et_____ spi- ri- ta-

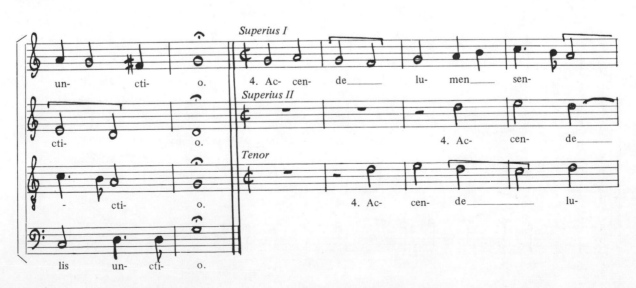

un- cti- o.   *Superius I*   4. Ac- cen- de_____ lu- men____ sen-

cti- o.   *Superius II*   4. Ac- cen- de_____

-cti- o.   *Tenor*   4. Ac- cen- de_____ lu-

lis un- cti- o.

44

Example 2—3

Example 3. *Pater superni luminis*

Example 3—2

Example 3–3

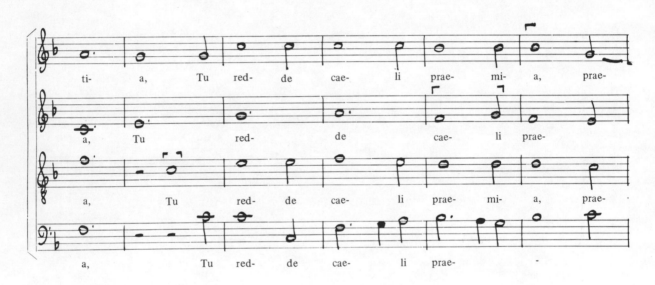

Example 4. Verses 1, 7 and 11 of *Magnificat Secundi toni*

Example 4—2

Example 4—3

Example 4—4

Example 4—5

Example 4—6

Example 4—7

(1) *In the print this is a semibreve and is preceded by both a semibreve and minim rest.*

55

Example 5. "Kyrie I" of *Missa Tu es Petrus*

56

Example 6. Sanctus of *Missa Tu es Petrus*

Example 6—2

Example 6—3

Example 6—4

cel- sis,   ho- san- na in ex- cel-   sis, in ex-

na in ex- cel-   sis, ho- san- na in ex- cel-

na in ex- cel- sis, ho- san- na in ex- cel-   sis, in ex-

in ex- cel-   sis,   ho- san-

cel- sis, in ex- cel- sis, ho- san- na in ex- cel-   sis, in ex-

cel- - sis.

sis, in ex- cel- sis.

cel- - sis.

na in ex- cel- sis.

cel- - sis.

Example 7. "Kyrie I" of *Missa Quarti toni*

Example 7—2

Example 8. Beginning of the Gloria of *Missa Quarti toni*

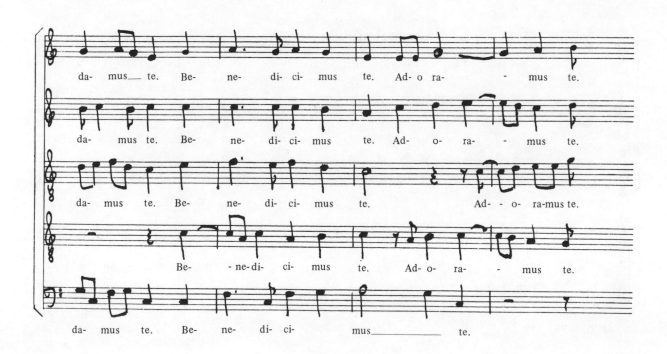

Example 9. Beginning of the Credo of *Missa Quarti toni*

Example 10. Kyrie of *Missa de Beata Virgine in Sabbato*

Example 10—2

Example 11. Beginning of the Gloria of *Missa de Beata Virgine in Sabbato*

Example 12. Beginning of the mirror canon in "Agnus II" of *Missa de Beata Virgine in Sabbato*

Example 13. Kyrie of *Missa Hoc est praeceptum meum*

Example 13—2

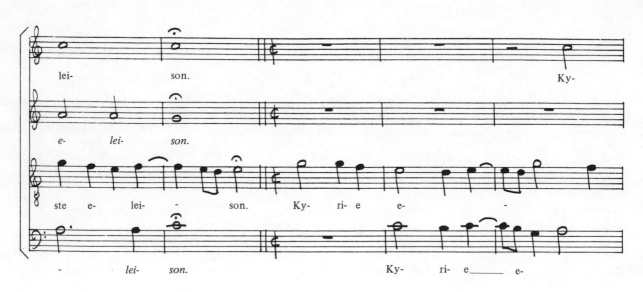

Example 14. Beginning of the Gloria of *Missa Hoc est praeceptum meum*

Example 15. "Et incarnatus" of *Missa Hoc est praeceptum meum*

Example 16. "Agnus II" of *Missa Hoc est praeceptum meum*

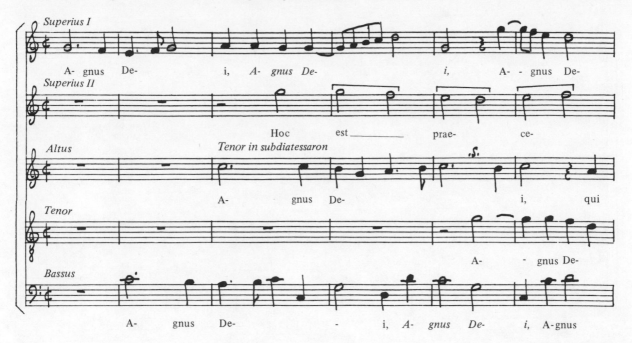

Example 16—2

Example 17. Beginning of the motet *Quasi cedrus* by Francisco Guerrero

Example 18. "Kyrie I" of *Missa Quasi cedrus*

Example 19. Beginning of the Gloria of *Missa Quasi cedrus*

Example 20. Beginning of the secunda pars of the motet *Quasi cedrus* by Francisco Guerrero

Example 21. Beginning of the Credo of *Missa Quasi cedrus*

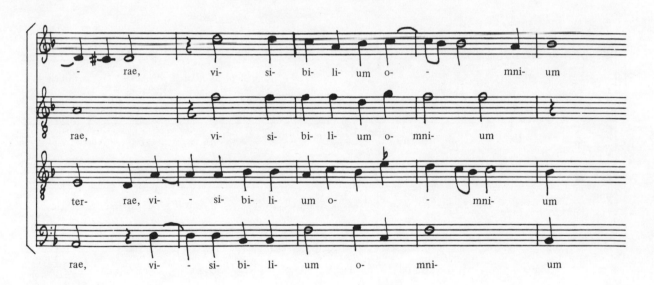

Example 22. Beginning of the Sanctus of *Missa Quasi cedrus*

Example 23. Beginning of the Agnus Dei of *Missa Quasi cedrus*

Example 24. Beginning of the motet *Hortus conclusus* by Rodrigo de Ceballos

Example 25. "Kyrie I" of *Missa Hortus conclusus*

Example 26. "Sanctus-Pleni" of *Missa Hortus conclusus*

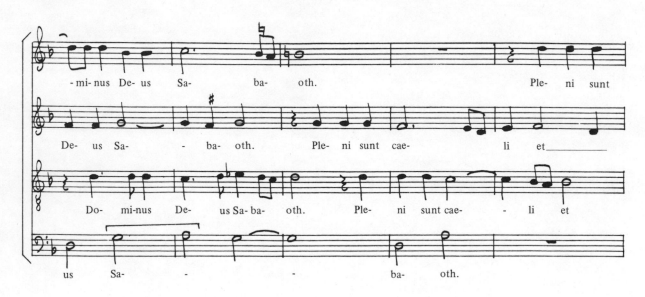

Example 26—2

Example 27. Beginning of the introit of *Missa pro defunctis*

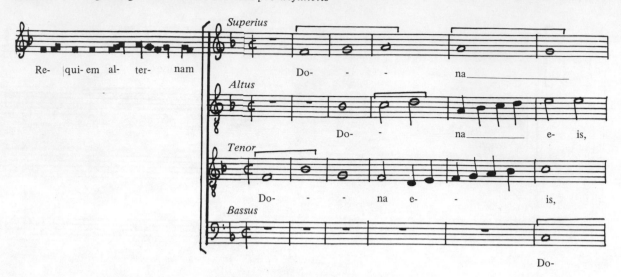

Example 28. "Sanctus" of *Missa pro defunctis*

Example 29. Beginning of the versicles from *Dies irae*

APPENDICES

APPENDIX I
THE DEDICATORY LETTER OF THE 1613 PRINT

PRAECLARISSIMO DOMINO FRATRI D.
PETRO PONZE DE LEON, ÇAMORENSI EPISCOPO
DIGNISSIMO, IOANNES ESQUIVEL ALMAE CIVITA-
TENSIS ECCLESIAE PORTIONARIUS, MUSI-
CAEQUE PRAEFECTUS. S. P. D.

Superioribus annis cum ad hanc regendam Ecclesiam, divina id efficiente gratia, assumptus esses, clarissime Praesul, universumque populum praecipua quadam amoris significatione tibi conciliasses, me imprimis tua animi mansuetudo, et lenitas sic sibi devinxit, ut te mihi in omnibus patronum, ac Mecoenatem iam inde elegerim. Cuius observantiae, et gratitudinis specimen aliquod cum enixe dare optarem, diuturni desiderii finem praesens fecit occasio. Volenti enim mihi volumen quoddam de concentu Ecclesiastico typis mandare, illudque alicuius Principis praesidio, recepta iam consuetudine, committere, non fuit diutius deliberandum; multae siquidem sese obtulerunt causae, quae me ad patrocinium tuum caeteris anteponendum facile perpulerunt. Considero namque tuae familiae antiquitatem: tuorum progenitorum pro amplificanda Christiana religione a sexcentis annis res bene gestas in mente revoco. Quas ex Granatensibus, Africanisque Mauris victorias feliciter reportaverint historiae ipsae haud obscure manifestant. Quibus denique praediis, quibus possessionibus multa Divorum Templa ditaverint, pia eorum, et religiosa monimenta testantur. Quae omnia cum ad veri Dei cultum, suorumque Regum fidelem operam revocata esse constet, inde factum est, ut non solum Archobrigae, Zarae, Martiae, Gadium, aliorumque oppidorum dominium merito obtinere, verum etiam Tolosanorum, Nabornensiumque Comitum insitam nobilitatem felici Legionis, et Aragoniae Regum affinitate cumulare meruerint. Sed quia haec in tantis temporum intervallis forte exoleta esse possent, mirum est dictu, quanto animi ardore, ac fortitudine his proximis annis excellentissimus Dux Rothericus frater tuus, caeteris totius Boeticae dynastis perterritis, ad pellendos Gadibus perfidos Anglos, Templorum et sacrarum virginum ulciscendas iniurias fulgentissima suorum subditorum stipatus caterva processerit: ita ut eius accelerationis fama hostes ipsos tantae virtutis stupore defixos ex pavida et direpta urbe potuerit exturbare. Ne autem quis te illis aliqua ex parte inferiorem ignoranter iudicet, divini numinis instinctu effectum fuisse credo, ut molli et delicata tunica cilicio, renitente purpura rudi, et aspero Dominicanae familiae vestitu commutata, arctiorem Religionis vitam elegeris: nam si illi inter tubarum clangorem, inter armorum strepitum, bombardaeque reboatum humanam, atque ideo fluxam et perituram gloriam, magna Hispanorum Regum Imperio accessione facta, sunt adepti, tu nequaquam his minora praestitisti: cum enim Regnum Coelorum vim pati ex assidua sacrarum Literarum lectione didiceris, illud expugnandum ratus, omni virtutum armatura munitus, operi te accinxisti: voluntaria siquidem paupertate contentus, inter continuas corporis verberationes, ciborum abstinentias, indefessas vigilias, propria privatus voluntate, publicis ad populum concionibus, privatis confessionum colloquiis, sic tibi, Christianoque gregi consuluisti, ut tuis laboribus gloriam non deficientem in coelis, et Regi Regum Christo innumeros filios te peperisse nemo dubitet. Cui igitur, cum haec vera sint, aptius, consultiusque mearum lucubrationum foetus divino Officio solemnius celebrando multo maiore, quam antea studio, et diligentia elaboratos, quam tibi destinare debui, cuius maioribus cultu, et observantia Deo omnium largitori debita nihil unquam aut charius aut antiquius fuisse minime dubia traditione accepimus, et qui totam vitae seriem, cunctasque actiones sic semper instituisti, ut Orthodoxae fidei augmento et propagationi, de tuae Religionis more, indefesse inservieris. Suscipe, igitur, praeclarissime Praesul, opusculum hoc Psalmorum, Hymnorum, Magnificarum, et Missarum modulus pro sui authoris tenuitate complectens, quod si sub amplissimi tui nominis protectione prodire patieris, satis cumulatum praemium labori meo persolutum esse arbitrabor. Quod reliquum est Dominationem tuam Deus Optimus Maximus ad sui nominis gloriam, Ecclesiaeque ornamentum quam diutissime tueatur incolumen.

APPENDIX II
THE TWO 1608 PRINTS OF JUAN ESQUIVEL

The earlier of Esquivel's two prints of 1608 was the volume of masses entitled *Missarum Ioannis Esquivelis in alma ecclesia Civitatensi portionarii et cantorum praefecti, liber primus. Superiorum permissu. Salmanticae ex officina typographica Arti Taberniel Antwerpiani, anno a Christo nato M.DC.VIII.* It appears in *RISM* A/I/2 as item E 825. The only copy cited there is a defective one preserved in the archives of the cathedral in Badajoz which lacks not only the title page and any introductory textual material the book once may have contained but also pages 1-2, 55-90 and 237-44. As can be seen from this copy, the last numbered page of the book is 253, the unnumbered verso of which contains the colophon: *Salmanticae excudebat Artus Tabernelius Antwerpianus XVI kalendas Marcias M.DC.IIX.*

Another copy once was owned by the Munich antiquarian Ludwig Rosenthal, who listed it as item 807 in his catalog 153. This copy served as the basis for the article by Albert Geiger cited in footnote 6. Its location is now unknown; perhaps it was destroyed during World War II. It seems to have been a complete copy and it is from this exemplar that the exact title of the volume is known since Geiger quoted it in his article. According to Geiger, this copy of the print lacked all reference to a dedication. The volume was, however, probably dedicated to the Virgin, with the dedication being expressed by an engraving on the title page depicting the composer kneeling before an altar above which hangs a painting of Mary holding the Infant Jesus. This engraving, as well as page 107 of the print, which contains four of the eight parts of the "Christe" of the *Missa hexachordum,* was reproduced by Geiger in his article and both were copied from there by Anglès for inclusion in his entry on Esquivel in *Die Musik in Geschichte und Gegenwart.*

The contents of the print are *Asperges me* (*a 4*), *Missa Ave, Virgo sanctissima* (*a 5*), *Missa Batalla* (*a 6*), *Missa hexachordum* (*a 8*), *Missa Ductus est Jesus* (*a 4*), *Missa Gloriose confessor Domini* (*a 4*), *Missa pro defunctis* (*a 5*) and *In paradisum* (*a 6*). The items which are incomplete in the Badajoz copy as a result of the loss of the various folios are *Asperges me, Missa Batalla* (the Kyrie is incomplete, the Gloria is missing entirely and the Credo is incomplete) and *Missa pro defunctis* (the Sanctus is incomplete, the Agnus Dei is missing entirely and the communion antiphon is incomplete). *Asperges me* is preserved in its entirety in the print of 1613, however, and it is possible to reconstruct the incipits of the missing or incompletely preserved movements of the *Missa Batalla* from the examples given by Geiger in his article.

Only one of the items in this print has yet been found in a manuscript source. This is the *Missa Ductus est Jesus,* which appears on folios 27*v*-36*r* in a codex owned by Octaviano Valdés, a canon of the cathedral of Mexico City; see Robert M. Stevenson, *Renaissance and Baroque Musical Sources in the Americas* (Washington: General Secretariat, Organization of American States, 1970), pp. 131-33. None of the items is available in a modern edition.

There also is only one copy of the motet volume of 1608 listed in *RISM* A/I/2 (item E 826). This is the copy preserved in the archives of the cathedral of Badajoz. It is defective and lacks not only the title page and all other preliminary textual material but also pages 1-2 and 269-71. Four of these, pages 2 and 269-71, contained music; page 1 must have contained the index and the colophon was on the back of page 271. Another copy, however, is preserved in the library of the Hispanic Society of America, in New York City. This copy, acquired from the Leipzig antiquarian Karl W. Hiersemann, who offered it for sale as item 251 in his catalog of 1911 entitled *Musik und Liturgie,* also is defective and everything preceding page 11 is missing as well as pages 107-10, 225-28, 255-56 and 263-66. Fortunately, the last page, 271, is present even though badly damaged and consequently the colophon, printed on the reverse of this page, has been preserved except for a few letters. It reads *[Sal]manticae excudebat [A]rtus Tabernelius [A]ntwerpianus quinto [k]alendas Iulii [M].DC.IIX.* According to Anglès, in his article on Esquivel in *Die Musik in Geschichte und Gegenwart,* another copy was discovered in the archives of the cathedral in Burgo de Osma in 1928 but no one other than Anglès has reported seeing it and whether it is still to be found there is uncertain. Nothing is known of its condition when discovered.

The Badajoz copies of both the masses of 1608 and the motets probably have belonged to the cathedral since from shortly after their publication. Nothing is known about the circumstances of their acquisition but one might conjecture that they perhaps were a gift or a legacy from Pedro Ponce de León, Esquivel's patron. In 1615, this prelate, while bishop of Zamora, was nominated to the see of Badajoz but it is uncertain whether he ever took possession of the diocese. Hernández Vegas, in his history of Ciudad Rodrigo, implies that he did but other sources state that he died in 1615, probably in December, before reaching Badajoz. If he did reach his new diocese it is quite possible that the copies of Esquivel's two prints of 1608 which are preserved there are those which the composer would have presented to his episcopal patron immediately upon their publication and which the bishop, in turn, gave or left as a legacy to the choir of the cathedral in Badajoz.

Because the title page has been lost from both the Badajoz and Hispanic Society copies of the motet print, we are dependent on Hiersemann's sale catalog of 1911 for an idea of what the exact title may have been. There the entry for the print reads "Esquivel, Juan, motecta festorum et dominicarum cum communi sanctorum, IV, V, VI et VIII vocilus [sic] concinnanda. Impreso en-fol. mayor (53 x 38 cm). Salmanticae excudebat Artus Tabernelius Antverpianus quinto calendarum Julii M.DC.IIX. (1608). Encuadernacion original de piel roja ornament. de hierros á frio, sobre madera." Since this copy of the print was among the many items which Hiersemann acquired from the private library of the then recently deceased Spanish musician and bibliophile Federico Olmeda, one can only assume that the copy had been provided with a title by Olmeda, who at some time must have encountered one which still retained its title page. Because Olmeda once served as chapelmaster of the cathedral in Burgo de Osma, one is tempted to assume that this was the copy reported by Anglès to be at the cathedral there in 1928. It should be noted that certain Spanish reference works cite this print as having been published in 1612 on the assumption that the form of the date which is used in the colophon, M.DC.IIX, is a misprint and should read M.DC.XII. That this is not the case is evident not only from the 1608 volume of masses by Esquivel but also from the volume of masses by Sebastián Vivanco which Tabernelius likewise published in 1608. In both of these Tabernelius indicated the year of publication on the title page as M.DC.VIII but in the colophon as M.DC.IIX.

The volume contains seventy-one items, forty-five of which are *a 4*, twenty-two *a 5*, three *a 6* and one *a 8*. All are motets except the last one, which is a reprint of the six-part ceremonial antiphon *In paradisum* with which the 1608 volume of masses also concluded. All are completely preserved in one or the other of the two copies except the opening item of the collection, *Salva nos, Domine*, which lacks that initial portion of its superius and tenor parts which appeared on page 2.

Sixty of the pieces in the print also are preserved in a late eighteenth-century manuscript choirbook in the archives of the cathedral in Plasencia (see Samuel Rubio, "El archivo de música de la Catedral de Plasencia," *Anuario Musical* 5 (1950), 147-68; Rubio designates this book as Ms. 1). Unfortunately, the motet *Salva nos, Domine* is not among those copied into the manuscript. Interestingly, however, the manuscript has a four-part setting of the "Et incarnatus est" section of the Credo immediately before the first of the Advent motets, *In illa die*. Because the same "Et incarnatus est" also appears as a manuscript addition immediately after this motet in the copy of the print owned by the library of the Hispanic Society, it seems probable that the Plasencia manuscript was made directly from this copy.

One of the motets in the print, *O vos omnes*, also is to be found in Livro de música number 12 in the library of the ducal palace in Vila Viçosa, Portugal. This is a manuscript of music for Holy Week which was copied in 1735 from books then in the music library assembled by King John IV of Portugal. It occurs on folios 18*v*-19*r*, between the Credo and Sanctus of a *Missa Dominicarum Adventus et Quadragessimae* by Manuel Cardoso, and has appended to it a secunda pars by Manuel Soares. See Manuel Joaquim, *Vinte livros de música polifónica do paço ducal de Vila Viçosa* (Lisbon: Fundação da Casa de Bragança, 1953), pp. 127 and 130.

Seven of Esquivel's motets have been published from the Plasencia manuscript in a practical modern edition by Samuel Rubio in his two-volume *Antología polifónica sacra* (Madrid: Editorial Conculso, 1954-1956). These are *Veni, Domine* (I:13), *Gloria in excelsis Deo* (I:27), *Emendemus in melius* (I:63), *O vos omnes* (I:215), *Ego sum panis vivus* (I:283), *Exaltata sum* (II:89) and *O quam gloriosum* (II:308). Of these, *Veni, Domine* and *Exaltata sum* are *a 5;* the others are all *a 4*. *Veni, Domine* recently was reprinted from the Rubio anthology in *Kalmus Study Score No. 708. The Spanish School* (New York: Edwin F. Kalmus, 1968), p. 90. Unfortunately, a number of Esquivel's accidentals were deleted by Rubio, apparently on the assumption that they had been added by the scribe who copied the Plasenica manuscript; consequently his edition of these works does not always reflect the composer's intentions.

APPENDIX III
EXTRACT FROM MATEO HERNÁNDEZ VEGAS,
CIUDAD RODRIGO. LA CATEDRAL Y LA CIUDAD

Escuelas de música. En nada fué tan decisiva la influencia de la Catedral, como en la enseñanza de la música. Ello fué debido a que nunca la Catedral confió esta enseñanza a personas extrañas, y principalmente al empeño constante de dar extraordinaria solemnidad al culto, llamando y dotando espléndidamente *a los mejores músicos que pudieran hallarse,* los cuales acudían a estos concursos de todas las regiones de España y aun del extranjero, como puede comprobarse por las actas capitulares. Puede asegurarse que todavía hoy la probada afición, el buen gusto y la extraordinaria aptitud de los mirobrigenses para el divino arte, obedecen a una tradición iniciada, sostenida e impulsada por las escuelas de música de la Catedral, regidas siempre por eminentes músicos.

La tradición arranca, por lo menos, del siglo XV, pues a 27 de Junio de 1494 fué elegido cantor y maestro de capilla el primer gran maestro de que se tiene noticia, llamado Giraldin Bucher, apellido que fué transformándose en Buxer, Buxel y Bujel, con que es conocido. Era natural de la Gascuña, de donde vino a Ciudad Rodrigo, atraído por las ricas raciones, que se ofrecían. Tan perito era en el arte, que, habiéndose casado aquí con una señora de noble linaje, con lo que se hizo incapaz del beneficio eclesiástico, el Cabildo le conservó la ración en forma de salario.

Entre sus muchos discípulos descolló su hijo Diego Bujel, autor de un libro de himnos, versos de claustro, etc., que regaló a la Catedral y se ha perdido. Fué primero niño de coro, contrajo matrimonio con una señora de la ilustre familia de los Aguilas, gozando la ración en forma de salario, como su padre, y últimamente, habiendo enviudado, se ordenó de sacerdote. Hizo las oposiciones a la *cantoria* con un Ramírez, a quien el Cabildo regaló ocho ducados de oro, de la vacante, para los gastos del viaje. A 30 de Noviembre de 1522, al salir de vísperas, "se da en encomienda a *Bucher* la media prebenda y media ración en la forma que la servía Altamirano."[1] Pocos días después el Cabildo da gratuitamente a Bucher la "casa en que vive, para que haga bien su oficio." A 13 de Enero de 1528, "porque es notoria su necesidad, se prestan 20 ducados al maestro de Capilla Diego Bucher." A 26 de Febrero de 1532, se señalan a Diego Bucher 2.000 maravedises de su prebenda. Item prestarle 50 ducados. Item daríe de balde, mientras sea maestro de capilla, la casa en que vive. Al dia siguiente jura no despedirse, mientras viva, para buscar otro partido de Catedral o Señor, salvo de persona real, etc.

---

[1] Altamirano habia sucedido a Giraldin Bucher.

Discípulo de Diego Bujel fué el no menos famoso Juan Cepa, natural de Descargamaría. Fué niño de coro de esta Catedral, haciéndose mención de él, como tal, por primera vez a 16 de Agosto de 1532. En Noviembre de 1547 todavía estaba en Ciudad Rodrigo, pues se le da "el ornamento bueno de brocado para ir a ser padrino en Robledillo." Ganó por oposición la ración de maestro de capilla de Málaga y después la de Ciudad Rodrigo, donde murió.

Abreviando esta relación, a Cepa sucedieron: El maestro Zuñeda, natural de Avila, maestro de capilla de Plasencia, de donde vino a Ciudad Rodrigo; Juan Navarro, natural de Marchena, famoso compositor, que tuvo primero la ración de Salamanca; Alonso de Velasco, que fué antes maestro de capilla de Santiago; el ilustre maestro Alonso de Tejada, que lo fué después de Toledo y Burgos; y, sobre todos, nuestro Juan Esquivel, el más eminente músico, que ha tenido la Catedral de Ciudad Rodrigo. Era natural de esta ciudad, mozo de coro de la Catedral y discípulo tan aventajado de Juan Navarro, que ganó todas las plazas a que oposító. Fué maestro y canónigo en Oviedo, de donde pasó a Calahorra, de allí a Avila y de Avila a Ciudad Rodrigo, de donde, por amor a su patria, ya no quiso salir. Cabañas, que vivió en su tiempo, cita los muchos libros que escribió y pondera su extraordinario mérito.

También en la ración de organista hubo en aquel tiempo eminentes maestros. Se distinguen: Los Valderas, padre e hijo; Hernán Ruiz de Segura, que luego fué contralto en Toledo; Alonso Gómez, hijo del célebre tenor del mismo nombre (naturales ambos de esta ciudad), que antes fué organista de Avila, Palencia y Plasencia, y finalmente, Pedro de Arguello, también natural de esta ciudad y discípulo de Gómez. Fué organista de Zamora, Osma y Palencia; y tal era su fama, que el Cabildo de Ciudad Rodrigo le llamó y le dió la ración, sin oponerse a ella.

De los capellanes de coro, dice Cabañas, que era uno de ellos: "Las demás raciones de cantores las han tenido hombres muy diestros y de admirables voces; y el querer yo escribir de cada uno en particular, sería proceder en infinito, y sólo digo que los que ahora tenemos este ministerio, que es oficio de ángeles, procuramos con nuestras voces alabar y reverenciar a este divino Señor, que es Dios, y a su Madre Santísima, para que a El y a ella merezcamos ver en los cielos por siempre jamás."

Es de advertir que estos capellanes de coro, no solamente habían de ser diestros en la música y canto y de admirables voces, sino que el Cabildo exigía que su cultura científica y literaria no desdijera de su cultura artística. Admira, en verdad, ver en las actas capitulares que para una capellanía, por ejemplo, de contrabajo, se exigieran ejercicios picando en las Decretales o en el Maestro de las Sentencias, con puntos de veinticuatro, etc; es decir, exactamente iguales a las modernas oposiciones mayores.

Del interés del Cabildo por conservar a grande altura su capilla de música, dan idea los siguientes datos que extractamos de las actas, omitiendo las fechas para abreviar: Encargar a Bucher que busque un contrabajo y un tiple; comisión a Robles y a Diego Bucher, para concertar cuatro trompetas, que tañan en las fiestas; traer ministriles altos (para esto ayudó el Ayuntamiento con 2.000 maravedises anuales, por acuerdo de 21 de Octubre de 1565); sacar a oposicones una capellanía de contrabajo, etc.; dar a Montoya 15 ó 16 ducados para un sacabuche; escribir al ilustre mirobrigense don Diego Guzmán y Silva, embajador de S. M. en Londres, para que envie de Inglaterra *diferencias de instrumentos de ministriles;* admitir *cheremías* y que den fianzas; comprar cornetas mutas, un sacabuche y una cheremía tiple; hacer dulzainas para un órgano de los grandes, etc., etc.

No es extraño que la capilla de música de la Catedral de Ciudad Rodrigo, además de asistir a todas las grandes solemnidades, sagradas y profanas, de la ciudad, fuera solicitada de lejanas tierras con el mismo fin. Así consta el haber asistido en distintas épocas a la fiesta de San Agustin, en Sanfelices; a Piedrahita, a la de la Visitación de Nuestra Señora; a Alcántara, con motivo de la canonización de San Pedro de Alcántara; a las fiestas de Almeida, en Portugal, etc.   (Volume I, pages 291-94)